THE
CONVERSION
CRISIS
A Continuing Discussion

THE CONVERSION CRISIS

A Continuing Discussion

Aharon Lichtenstein • J. David Bleich
Abraham Carmel • S. Zevulun Lieberman
Mark D. Angel • Shlomo Riskin
J. Simcha Cohen • Moshe Yeres
Michael J. Broyde • Shmuel Kadosh
Avi Sagi • Zvi Zohar

Edited by
Emanuel Feldman and Joel B. Wolowelsky

KTAV / The Rabbinical Council of America

Library of Congress Cataloging-in-Publication Data

Conversion crisis (2011)
  The conversion crisis : a continuting discussion / edited by Emanuel
Feldman and Joel Wolowelsky.
     p. cm.
  ISBN 978-1-60280-161-5
  1. Conversion--Judaism. I. Feldman, Emanuel, 1927-. II. Wolowel-
sky, Joel B. III. Title.
  BM729.P7C66 2011
  296.7'14--dc22

                    2011008638

Distributed by
KTAV Publishing House, Inc.
888 Newark Avenue
Jersey City, N.J. 07306
Email: orders@ktav.com

CONTENTS

FOREWORD

A shorter version of this volume appeared twenty years ago under the title *The Conversion Crisis*. At that time, as Rabbi Feldman indicated in his introduction, the sense of crisis derived from an increase in intermarriage and the subsequent pressure to recognize large numbers of non-Jews as Jewish who lacked the religious commitment necessary for classical conversion to Judaism, leading in turn, to the potential erosion of halakhic standards.

During the intervening years, the aforementioned pressures and the dangers of perfunctory, irresponsible conversions have not abated. The situation has become even more complicated because some alarmed rabbinical authorities have championed more rigid safeguards in screening both converts and the rabbinic courts that oversee and ratify conversions.

Beyond the practical halakhic controversies, conversion has become a critical question for Jewish thought as well. Many modern people regard religious identity as one cultural option among others, defined, adopted and shed at will like other consumer preferences. Not only is such an outlook inhospitable to the absolute, irrevocable commitment essential to Judaism. It is also intolerant of the idea that absolute, irrevocable commitment to a religious community is achieved through public engagement in particular legally binding acts that constitute conversion, as set down by religious law and its institutions. Contemporary liberalism tends to universalize and impose its perceptions wherever it holds sway: this leads to an insistence that becoming a Jew, unlike becoming a citizen of a political state, is simply a matter of choice rather than formal conversion. Consequently, Jews living in Western societies are increasingly compelled to formulate what it means for a Jew to define conversion in terms of binding halakhic communal norms. Understanding conversion thus becomes essential to understanding Judaism.

The articles reprinted here pertain to both aspects of the conversion crisis. Most take positions on contemporary halakhic problems. Some, most notably the opening essay by our revered mentor R. Aharon Lichtenstein, are concerned with the place of conversion within a broader Jewish theology. As he puts it, the entrance to Jewish existence partakes of, and corresponds to, the reality of Jewish life as the gateway foreshadows the home.

We have added two recent contributions. Michael Broyde's review of Avi Sagi and Zvi Zohar's *Transforming Identity: The Ritual Transition from Gentile to Jew–Structure and Meaning* subjects to halakhic critique their creative attempt to reorder the Talmudic literature on conversion and to revise, in its light, much of the subsequent halakhic debate, downplaying the emphasis on religious commitment. Sagi and Zohar in turn, have taken the opportunity to present their positions in our pages.

The Conversion Crisis

As with all *Tradition* productions, it is a duty and pleasure to thank the Rabbinical Council of America, whose constant support makes our publication possible. Special thanks to the RCA's Executive Vice–President Rabbi Basil Herring, who has sustained *Tradition's* existence and integrity during my years as Editor, and to our Associate Editor, Dr Joel Wolowelsky, who initiated this collection.

This volume lays no claim to halakhic or theological exhaustiveness or authoritativeness. If it succeeds in clarifying the subject and provoking further thought we will be more than satisfied.

Shalom Carmy
Editor

INTRODUCTION

Conversions into Judaism have not played a major role in Jewish history, and, in fact, the laws of conversion in the halakhic literature consist of only two succinct chapters in the *Shulhan Arukh*, (Yoreh Deah 268-9). When conversions did occur, the halakhic procedures were universally accepted by all Jews: total sincerity in the convert's desire to become a Jew, with no ulterior motives, acceptance of Judaism without reservations, study and knowledge of basic Jewish beliefs and practices, ritual circumcision and immersion in a *mikveh* before a properly constituted *bet-din* (rabbinic court).

But this was once upon a time. Today, conversion to Judaism has itself been converted into a major issue of Jewish life. The open society, Jewish mobility, and loosening family ties – among other factors – have caused a serious slippage in Jewish learning and commitment, resulting in a blurring of differences between Jews and non-Jews, an upsurge in marriages between them, and a concomitant proliferation of conversions into Judaism, fueled primarily by such marriages. The small section of the *Shulhan Arukh* dealing with *gerut* looms large in contemporary times.

Of course, the unfortunate fact is that the classic halakhic conversion procedures are no longer insisted upon outside of Orthodoxy, and a large number of today's conversions are performed simply to appease families or to salve consciences, and if truth be told, cannot be described as anything other than papered-over intermarriages. All too often, these conversions have not fulfilled basic halakhic norms: commitment to mitzvah observance is not demanded, Jewish knowledge is not required, and in many cases mikveh immersion is not practiced.

To be sure, in this age of convenient conversions, there are still to be found true proselytes who come into Judaism in the accepted manner, who convert because of deep commitment and yearning, who are a pride and joy to *am Yisrael*, and whose loyalty and sacrifice uplift and inspire other Jews. But tragically, the vast majority of converts today–through no fault of their own–are, halakhically speaking, of highly questionable Jewish status. This obviously has grave implications for the future of the total Jewish community.

This situation has exacerbated tensions between halakhic Judaism and the rest of the Jewish community, providing grist for the canard that the Orthodox rabbinate refused to acknowledge such conversions because it does not accept the Jewishness of anyone who is not Orthodox. The fact is, of course, that when a halakhic conversion process is bypassed and subverted, halakhic integrity demands that such procedures not be accepted, no matter who the presiding rabbi is.

The Conversion Crisis

The essays offered here have all appeared in *Tradition: A Journal of Orthodox Jewish Thought*, published by the Rabbinical Council of America. They are part of an honest attempt to define the parameters of an issue which has so many serious ramifications for the future of Jewry. They are offered here not as the definitive rulings of *psak halakhah*, nor do they bear the imprimatur of Orthodox Judaism in general or of the Rabbinical Council of America in particular. Rather, they are tentative explorations designed to reconnoiter the territory, and to help clarify the central issues involved. While the essays are written from a variety of perspectives, one unifying thread binds them together: a fealty and commitment to the integrity of the classical halakhah, and to its authority.

I express my deepest thanks to my predecessor, Rabbi Walter Wurzburger, under whose distinguished quarter–century editorship of *Tradition* most of these essays were originally published; to Rabbi Benjamin Walfish, Executive Vice-President of the Rabbinical Council of America, whose constant support helps make possible the publication of our journal; and to Dr. Joel B. Wolowelsky, an associate editor of *Tradition*, who helped bring this volume to publication.

It is our hope that these essays will serve to inform, guide, and instruct, and that, without polemics or apologetics, they will help illuminate some of the darkness which presently envelopes this crucial matter.

Emanuel Feldman
Editor, *Tradition*

ON CONVERSION
Aharon Lichtenstein

The status of *gerut* as a subject of discussion and debate is not a recent phenomenon. For ages, indeed millennia, this topic has been implicated in a broad range of problems. Some authorities are disturbed by the option of *gerut per se*. This is especially so of those who stress the unique, inborn holiness that characterizes the Jew. To cite but a few instances, the ability of a non–Jew to convert precipitated a variety of difficulties and objections for Rabbi Yehudah Halevi, the Maharal of Prague, and the School of Habad.

Quite apart from this primary issue, however, the problems can be further subdivided. First, how is one to treat a candidate for Judaism? This question has practical consequences in determining the actual conversion process. Shall we pursue the proselyte or avoid him? Repel with the left hand while attracting with the right, or vice versa? Second, how should we relate to the *ger* after his conversion? Needless to say, the possibility of derision is out of the question; the Torah explicitly admonishes us: "And the *ger* you shall not deride nor oppress."[1] And the rabbis state: "He who derides the *ger* violates three negative commandments";[2] R. Eliezer the Great enumerates thirty–six distinct places, and according to one opinion, forty–six, where the Torah forewarns us to respect the *ger*.[3]

But beyond this, how to assess the nature of the *ger* and his integration into the Nation of Israel is unclear, and perhaps in dispute. Encouragement on the one hand and repulsion on the other; some esteem the *ger*, while others approach him with cautious apprehension.

However, the issue of relating to the *ger* is not the one I wish to address. My focus is on the process of *gerut*, the phenomenon in itself. If we wish to define and describe *gerut*, we will discover that its essence is in its being a turning point. The foundation of *gerut* is a radical transformation: an uprooting from one world to strike root in a different one.

This point specifically characterizes Jewish conversion and distinguishes it, historically, from parallel movements in the classical world. As Arthur Darby Nock emphasized, whereas adoption of one of the religions that dominated the Hellenistic world, such as Orphism or Mithraism, meant merely a supplement to the local tradition and not its total negation, Judaism (and, consequently, Christianity) presents conversion as a total metamorphosis. The *ger* is compelled to abandon his past background and enter the realm of his future, for commitment to Judaism is based on Elijah's question: "How much longer will you oscillate, wavering between two options?"[4] In the words of Nock, conversion demands "renunciation and a new beginning. What was required was not merely the acceptance of ritual, but rather a willful attachment to a theology; in a word, faith: a new life in a new nation."[5]

1

This should not cause surprise. *Gerut,* after all, embodies, nay constitutes, the forging of a covenant that is, by its very nature, exclusive: "…And the two of them made a covenant"[6] – to the exclusion of others. Nonetheless, the question still arises: What type of turning point? How does it take effect, and in what manner is it realized and manifested?

It seems to me that in *gerut,* both in the process and in the outcome, there exist two elements that are to some extent parallel, to some extent complementary, and to some extent contradictory.[7] On the one hand, *gerut* is grounded in a profound revolution. In its ideal form, its root is a longing for holiness, its core, desire for the *Ein Sof,* gravitation to a sublime and exalted ethic, striving for a world wholly good and wholly true. "David called himself a *ger,* as it is said:[8] 'I am a stranger *(ger)* in the land.'"[9] Of course, he was not a *ger* in the strict halakhic sense (although he was descended from proselytes); but in the realm of religious experience, he had penetrated the soul of the *ger* and related to it: "As a hart panting after water brooks, so my soul pants after You."[10] Here is the essence of *gerut*: a craving that dislodges one from the society of one's youth and finds expression in the overcoming of the confines of group and nation.

To be sure, the source and character of this element are apt to change. In certain cases, its essence is reaction to a sullied past, a renunciation of a life filled with iniquity or deprived of meaning and purpose. In this form, *gerut* is included in *teshuvah* (repentance); it is precipitated by regret over the past, abandonment of sin, and resolve for the future. At other times, the motive propelling the proselyte is the glow of the future, not the sordidness of the present. The potential *ger,* despite being in a setting that is not necessarily defiled, but merely defective, sees himself as isolated, "in a dry and thirsty land, without water." In his anguish he pleads: "O God, You are my God, earnestly I seek You: my soul thirsts for You, my flesh longs for You."[11] On the practical level, as the Rambam put it, the *ger* desires "to enter the covenant and to be absorbed under the divine aegis, and to accept for himself the yoke of the Torah."[12] But categorizing the different types of *gerut* is merely a matter of detail. The fundamental motive is one: a religious experience, a spiritual effervescence – sometimes feverish, oft-times tranquil; in short, the birthpangs of a Jewish soul. This creation is private and personal–if you will, even subjective. Essentially, it is the *ger*'s intimacy with the Holy One. "The king has brought me into his chamber," and no stranger will trespass into the inner sanctum. Nothing is more a matter of the heart than *gerut,* and, in the channels of the heart, can there be room for external involvement?

This principle finds expression in a simple, yet famous, Halakhah: "A *ger* is like a newborn babe."[13] We customarily associate this statement with several laws: a *ger* is not aligned genealogically to his father, nor does he inherit from him (by biblical injunction); and, according to Resh Lakish, he does not fulfill the commandment to be fruitful and multiply through children born to him while he was a Gentile.[14] However, these are only consequences; it behooves us to understand and grasp the concept itself, in its literal context. The *ger* returns to the source, penetrating the secrets of ontological reality, and, while standing on the threshold of a new life, ruminates over the mystery of existence and is involved in a superior creation: he is born and gives birth at once.

The validity of this comparison is pronounced (albeit with an emphasis on the "converter" more than on the convert) in its aggadic formulations: "Whoever brings another person under the wings of the *Shekhinah* is considered as having created him, shaped him, and brought him into the world."[15] To be sure, this refers to the educator of a Jewish child, but how much the more does it apply to *gerut*. In the well-known words of the *Sifre* regarding Avraham our Patriarch: "And you shall love… like the love of humanity that Avraham your forefather had, as it is written: 'and the souls that they had acquired in Haran.' Now if all people united to create a small gnat and give it a soul, they would not succeed. What then does this verse mean? It teaches that Avraham was converting people and bringing them into the Jewish faith."[16] And in Bereshit Rabbah, the same passage concludes: "Rather, to teach us that one who brings the non-Jew closer to Judaism and converts him, it is as if he had created him."[17]

So far we have only been dealing with only one aspect of *gerut*: subjective and intimate, confined to the relationship of the *ger* to his Creator, centered around an internal experience and spiritual nascence, linked to *teshuvah*, which, in the Rambam's celebrated formulation, is also defined as a personal metamorphosis and new creation symbolized by birth ("And he alters his name, as if to say: I am another, and I am not the same person that committed those deeds").[18]

However, there is a second aspect to *gerut*: objective, formal, communal. If the *ger* is a partner in the dialogue taking place in the depths of his soul, he simultaneously becomes the subject of public assessment, participating – albeit, to be sure, not in an emotional vacuum – in a crystallized ceremony. Here, the emphasis is not upon process, including all the adventures and apprehension implied in the word, but on procedure. To his knocking on the door, he hears a response, to wit: Let us presume that your spiritual pilgrimage has prepared you sufficiently for *gerut*; but if you want to achieve it, you must follow these steps in order to be accepted.

This element, too, finds expression and symbolic representation in a Halakhah. "Rabbi Hiyya bar Abba said in the name of Rabbi Yohanan: A *ger* requires the presence of three people, for *mishpat* [judicial process] is written with reference to a *ger*."[19] For the same reason, since Halakhah deems *gerut* a form of legal procedure, conversion cannot take place at night;[20] and the Rambam saw this as the source of the gemara's prohibition against the *ger*'s ritual immersion (*tevilah*) on a Sabbath or a holiday: "Since *gerut* requires a *bet din*, we immerse the *ger* neither on a Sabbath nor on a holiday nor at night; although if he was immersed, then he is a *ger*."[21] This is not merely a matter of supernumerary piety. In the opinion of some commentators, led by the Ramban,[22] *tevilah* at night is ineffective even *post factum*. Even according to the Rambam, we may assume, as did the *Maggid Mishneh*, that it is valid *a posteriori* only because, in certain cases, juridical procedures may be concluded at night.[23] This assumption is clearly borne out by the Rambam's formulation with respect to the need for three judges: "If he immersed privately, and converted with no witnesses, or even in front of two persons, he is not a *ger*."[24] Many Rishonim took issue with him on this point and sanctioned private *tevilah*–this, however, not because they valued the necessity of a *bet din* any less, but because they deemed a *bet din*'s presence as mandatory only at the time that the *ger* accepts the normative onus of *mizvot*, and not during the immersion ceremony.[25] As for the requirement of having a *bet din* at one of the stages of *gerut,* all commentators – with the exception of one opinion quoted by Tosafot[26] – recognized it as indispensable; *gerut* consists of an actual *din*, a judge and his subject.

Between the elements of birth and adjudication, there are two distinctions that are completely separate from a logical standpoint–in fact, one could probably find one in the absence of the other–but that actually tend to arise concomitantly. Until now, I have accentuated one point, that of process–spiritual and private on the one hand, formal and communal on the other. Beyond this, however, the goal differs no less than the path. Birth emphasizes a spiritual creation; the legal aspect, a social affiliation. The potential *ger* appears on society's rostrum and presents himself as a candidate for citizenship in "the kingdom of priests and the holy nation," knocking not only on Heaven's door but also on the gates of *Knesset Yisrael*, the Jewish people. He is not content with being brought by the king into his chamber; the *ger* strives, as well, to "climb the date palm and take hold of its twigs."[27]

Our initial consideration of the two features of *gerut* certainly inclines us to see the yearning of the potential *ger* as the essence of *gerut,* and the judicial process as merely a validation, an endorsement. To a degree, this inclination is correct, but only to a degree. The legal aspect of *gerut* and the attachment to *Knesset Yisrael* involved in it are not solely an issue of a seal of approval. *Knesset Yisrael* does not merely mediate between the *ger* and the Almighty. She is a participant, and not just a broker; a concerned party, and not just an agent of God. In the encounter of the I and Thou that is established through *gerut,* the *ger* meets two Thous: The Lord of the Universe, and His nation, Israel. Not, God forbid, the latter alone; this would border on idolatry. Surely he confronts *Knesset Yisrael* solely in the light of its being "holy unto God, the first of His harvest." In this context, however, there is a very real encounter.

This point is reflected in the very procedures of *gerut*, especially as the Rambam delineated them:

> How are *gerim* accepted? When one comes from the Gentiles to be converted to Judaism, and [the *bet din*] finds no pretext [for his conversion], they say to him: "What has led you to such conversion? Don't you know that Israel is at present afflicted, oppressed, attacked, preyed upon, and that misfortunes befall her?" If he responds, "I know, and I am not worthy," they accept him immediately.[28]

The question arises: What is the nature of this declaration? It is mentioned in the gemara,[29] but there it can be understood as a part of the investigation to determine the sincerity of the *ger*. However, the Rambam here is explicitly dealing with the stage at which the *ger*'s sincerity has already been demonstrated. If so, why is this lengthy discourse needed?

Actually, the answer is quite simple. Let us ask ourselves what would happen if a potential *ger* were to declare himself ready to accept every one of the 613 commandments, committing himself to rigorous observance of the *mizvot*, minor as well as major, but refused to accept any sort of attachment to the nation, even the most minimal degree of allegiance. He does not wish to share in its present adversities, does not identify with its past, and does not yearn for its future. What is his status? We may answer unequivocally, on the basis of the Rambam's words in the *Hilkhot Teshuvah*. Among the transgressors who, "for their tremendous wickedness and sinfulness," do not inherit a share in the world–to–come the Rambam counts "those who separate themselves from the ways of society." And characteristically he details:

> He who separates himself from the [Jewish] people, although he may never have violated a law, if he stands aloof from the community of Israel, and does not participate in their communal observances, or share in their calamities, or fast on their fasts, but instead goes his own way like any member of the local [non–Jewish] populace, as if he were not one of them: no share in the world–to–come awaits him.[30]

This being so, the verdict in our case is crystal–clear: there has not been a total, comprehensive acceptance of *ol mizvot*. The prospective *ger* has readily committed himself to the entire Torah, only excluding involvement in the community, but this exclusion is hardly a trivial matter.

In light of this decision, we no longer need to wonder about the declaration concerning Israel's situation at the *gerut*. It is not solely an inquest into the motivation for conversion. The declaration by the *bet din* is a stage in the fulfillment of *gerut per se* and relates to the commitment implicit in it.

In this context, the individual and the community encounter each other along a very wide front. The *ger* does not meet and identify with the present nation alone, but with its past and future as well. Once again, it is the Rambam who underscores this point. The Mishnah states:

> The *ger* must bring [his first fruits], but he does not utter [the accompanying declaration], for he cannot say "that God has sworn to our fathers to give us"; and if his mother was Jewish, he brings [the first fruits] and utters [the declaration]. And when [the *ger*] prays privately, he says "the Lord of Israel's forefathers"; and when he is in the synagogue, he says "the Lord of your forefathers."[31]

In contrast, the Rambam rules in accordance with the view of R. Yehudah in the Jerusalem Talmud:

> The *ger* himself brings [the first fruits] and makes the declaration. Why? [God said to Avraham:] "For I have made you a father unto a multitude of nations": hitherto you were the father of Aram, and herewith you are the father of all nations.[32]

And, in the Rambam's own words:

> The *ger* brings [the first fruits] and makes the declaration, since it was spoken to Avraham, "I have made you a father unto a multitude of nations"; here he was made the patriarch of everyone in the world who [ever] becomes Jewish.[33]

In this formulation, the opinion of R. Yehudah does not identify the *ger* with a specific history, for it is possible to view the attachment to Avraham as direct, exclusive of mediation through *Knesset Yisrael*. If so, one may ask (as the Ramban already hinted),[34] that while the mention of Avraham is understandable, how can a *ger* describe Yizhak and Yaakov as his forefathers? The Rambam dealt with this issue in his famous responsum to R. Ovadiah Ger Tzedek. He opens with an explanation in keeping with the thrust of his words in the Mishneh Torah:

> The fundamental point here is that it was Avraham our father who instructed the nation, enlightening them and informing them of the true faith, and of God's unity and singularity. It was he who repudiated idol worship and violated its worship, nullifying it, bringing many to accept God, teaching and instructing them, commanding his sons and future descendants after him to remain faithful to the Way of God, as it says in the Torah: "For I know him, that he will command his children and his household after him, and they shall keep the way of the Lord." Therefore all who embrace Judaism until the end of all generations, and all who profess the unity of the Lord's Name as is directed in the Torah, are like the pupils of Avraham of blessed memory and are members of his household, all of them; it was he who brought them to this positive juncture, and, as he did with the members of his own generation by dint of his skill at oratory and teaching, so he has reclaimed everyone who will convert in the future, through the testament he left his children and his descendants. As a result, Avraham our forefather was the father of his legitimate progeny who follow the path forged by him, and he is also the father of every *ger* who converts.

Up to this point, the Rambam has discussed the direct link to Avraham; on the basis of his thesis, he concludes:

> But [as for saying] "You [God] took us out of Egypt" or "[God] performed miracles for our ancestors," if you want to change the wording and say "You took Yisrael out of Egypt," or "the miracle You wrought for Israel," say it [however you please].

But then he goes a step further:

> And if you do not change [the wording], there is no loss whatsoever, for after having entered the Jewish fraternity and accepted Judaism, there is no difference between you and us, and all the miracles that were wrought were wrought for us and for you. This is Isaiah's intention in the verse: "Neither let the son of the stranger, that has joined himself to the Lord, speak, saying, 'The Lord has surely separated me from His people.' "[35] There is no difference or incongruity between you and us in any respect.[36]

The words are self–explanatory: in the aftermath of his admission into *Knesset Yisrael*, the *ger* identifies with its past, its triumphs as well as its failures, no less than he does with the present; with eschatological vision as with current vibrant reality. The *ger* is born both as a servant of God and as a citizen of the nation, and hence the appropriateness of a *bet din* to judge and accept him.

We can, if we wish, discern the duality of *gerut* reflected in various manifestations over the generations. If we focus on the process of *gerut,* we may note three prominent phases. The first is symbolized by Avraham Avinu. Avraham, our rabbis informed us, is called "the forerunner of *gerim*"[37] – and not merely in a symbolic sense. The Mekhilta describes Avraham's circumcision as an actual proselyte's *berit milah*, not only as a fulfillment of God's command.[38] Clearly, Avraham's *gerut* highlights the first aspect of *gerut*. It is an individual process in toto, for it is characterized by singularity. He is lonely by nature. "Avraham was a *yahid*–Avraham was singular," exclaims the gemara.[39] The significance of this quality is further stressed in the well–known adage by which Rabbi Yehudah interpreted Avraham's title *Ivri*–"the whole world on one side, and he alone on the other."[40] When was he more solitary than at his conversion? His *gerut* was conducted purely on the level of a direct attachment to the Creator, striving and yearning for the Absolute, and following a direct divine bidding: "And the Lord said to Avraham, 'And you shall observe My covenant, you and your descendants after you for all their generations.' "[41] This verse introduces the commandment of *milah,* but in its original context, it was an injunction for *gerut.* This *gerut* is exclusively birth, *it'aruta di-letata ve-it'aruta di-le'ela* – "arousal from below and arousal from above," but without brokers. Neither judge nor judicial procedure; only the birth of a world and the creation of a soul. It is epitomized in an interpretation by the Midrash Tanhuma on the verse "and I shall make you a great nation": " 'I will transform you' is not the word chosen here, but 'make,' for I am creating in you a new person, similar to what is said: 'and God *made* the heavens, and God *made* the two lights.' "[42]

The second stage consists of a singular phenomenon: the period from the exodus from Egypt to the revelation at Sinai. Here, of course, the communal dimension of *gerut* was added: the Torah portrays the day of *mattan Torah* as a "Day of Assembly."[43] The meaning of that *gerut* is not exhausted merely in attachment to the Creator, but includes the formation of a "righteous nation that keeps faithfulness."[44] The legal charter, however, is missing. There is neither a judging nor a judged congregation; rather, a people standing together on the threshold of emergence into the world, and entering, without mediator or midwife, the world of eternal life as the lot of God's inheritance.

However, what transpired at Sinai was a unique event. From that time on, in the third stage, the *ger* requires both birth and *mishpat* in order to identify with *Knesset Yisrael* even as he clings to the Sovereign of the universe. Within this framework, although both components are compulsory, there may, in all likelihood, be certain cases wherein the social aspect is primary. If Avraham Avinu is the *ger* of birth par excellence, we may perceive another biblical convert as a prototype for a predominantly legal–social conversion. This element is symbolized by Ruth, not so much because of the emphasis upon formal procedure as because of the stress on interpersonal union as the impetus behind *gerut.* Doubtless, she unconditionally accepted upon herself the yoke of the Torah and *malkhut shamayim*–"and your God is my God." But from the biblical text it is quite clear, most significantly, that she was animated by love for Naomi, and through Naomi for all Israel: "And Ruth said. 'Entreat me not to leave you.' "[45] The source of the internal pressure is bared to all. This point is similarly stressed in what Boaz says. "And Boaz answered and said to her, 'It has been fully related to me, all that you have done to your mother–in–law since your husband's death: how you left your father, your mother, and the land of your birth, and went to a people unknown to you before.' " Only in the next sentence does he mention the purely spiritual element: "May God reward your deed, and may it be a full reward from God, the Lord of Israel, under whose wings you have come to seek refuge."[46]

Whatever the examples, the central fact for us today is that, since Sinai, there has been an intrinsic dualism in the framework of *gerut:* spiritual nativity as a servant of God on a certain level, together with standing for judgment as servant and peer.[47] The Halakhah insists upon both aspects. In keeping with the general spirit of Halakhah, the internal experience alone does not suffice. Contrary

7

to the modern Zeitgeist, which tends to define religion as a purely subjective reality, Halakhah strives to interweave the external and the internal. Wary of founding the spiritual life upon castles in the air, Halakhah relies upon defined actions and firm limits–and demands them. Even in a nonsocial framework, Hazal assumed, almost axiomatically, the necessity of an objective act in *gerut*. "And [according to] Rabbi Yehoshua," asks the gemara, "where do we see that the matriarchs performed *tevilah*?" The answer is immediate: "It is dictated by logic: for in its absence, how could they have become Jewesses at all?"[48]

If this is the case with the matriarchs, then all the more so after the giving of the Torah, when *gerut* has assumed the added dimension of entrance into *Knesset Yisrael*. One need hardly stress, however, that integration into the nation, be it rooted in the most sublime self–dedication, is insufficient. *Gerut* means, first and foremost, a religious–spiritual turning. The procedure of *gerut* comes in the wake of such a transformation, but not in its stead. The conversion consists of formal stages, but they are not *pro forma*. Moreover, the Halakhah stresses the interlacing of this turning into the actual act of *gerut*. Acceptance of the laws must occur twice: once before the *tevilah*, at which time, according to the Rambam, the *bet din* discourses at length on the tenets of Judaism, "the unity of God and the prohibition against idolatry,"[49] and also informs the convert of some of the more lenient and more stringent commandments; and again during the *tevilah*, when "three stand over him and inform him of some of the lenient commandments and some of the strict commandments a second time while he stands in the water."[50] What is the nature of this second declaration? Are we worried that the *ger's* commitment has lapsed in so short a time? It is solely in order to weave the acceptance of the *mizvot* into the act of *tevilah*, to supply the *tevilah* with the specific character of a *tevilah* of *gerut*, to integrate the spiritual intent with the formal act.

It would be pleasant to assume that there is no conflict between these two themes; that the selfsame act effectively subsumes both domains. A single *tevilah* is doubly efficacious. It climaxes protracted spiritual birth, culminating in emergence into the Jewish world, and, as definitive judgment, confers citizenship of *Knesset Yisrael*. Thus it serves simultaneously as the apex of a spiritual pilgrimage and as the essence of a social quest.

This would be agreeable, but I doubt whether so flattering an assumption can be conscientiously maintained. We should not make light of the difference between these two factors. Each is distinct in its very essence: one rooted in nature, the other in legality. Of course, birth too, even in its biological form, constitutes a phenomenon that concerns Halakhah; it is defined and quantified: the emergence of most of the fetus, of its head, its forehead,[51] and, according to the Rambam, even of most of its forehead, is an actual halakhic measurement.[52] This, however, is nothing more than coincidental. Intrinsically, birth lies outside of the juridical field, except that the law must pass judgment upon it. *Gerut*, however, is actual *mishpat*, and here lies the duality. This duality may in fact become, especially in today's prevalent mood, antinomy–and not only according to the individualistic romantic view that stresses the contradiction between law and nature and emphasizes absolute privacy in the spiritual realm. Even a traditional sensibility appreciates the breaching of the sanctum when the *ger* bares his innermost soul *coram populo,* with three strangers present in the delivery room. Recognizing and valuing modesty, it encourages concealment over revelation. Itself a "spring shut up, a fountain sealed,"[53] it senses that the juridic presence and framework are likely to undermine the religious–aesthetic moment at that most sublime instant. The *ger* is eager to soar–and three judges clip his wings, subjecting him to their examination.[54] In candor, we must further admit that the combination of these two factors may produce paradoxical results. Suffused with an effervescence and longing that characterize the end of a lengthy internal struggle and a supreme purification, the *ger* may stand trial in front of judges (even laymen according to some)[55] possessing a routine if not indifferent religious sensibility. In his heart, burning fire; in theirs, perhaps dimming embers.

Nevertheless, the Halakhah insists on the need for birth and *mishpat* together, and with good reason. The duality of *gerut* is not an isolated fact. It is an inherent part of the fundamental duality of religious life in general. The life of the devout, both in its universal form and, to a sharper degree, in its specifically Jewish form, is also dual. On the one hand, it is purely the realm of the individual: the sanctum sanctorum, innermost of the innards. Within the man of faith, as Rav Soloveitchik stressed in his essay, loneliness reverberates.[56] His relation to the Creator takes place in intimacy. His ideal experience is, in the famous words of Plotinus, "the flight of the alone to the alone."[57] "Religion," said Whitehead, "is solitariness…. If you are never solitary, you are never religious."[58] But on the other hand, religion has always developed in a congregational setting. Its historical existence is dependent at every stride and step on communal ritual and shared faith. This cannot be explained solely in the manner of Durkheim and his school, who view society as the source of religion, in the sense that religion grows and develops only in response to social needs and demands, so that, in the final analysis, it is society itself that is served in one form or another.[59] This doctrine is open to criticism even from a purely sociological standpoint. I, for one – far from an expert in the field – am inclined to accept Malinowski's contention that Durkheim's approach ignores some important phenomena, and may even be based on a distorted sense of some fundamental concepts.[60] In any case, from a Jewish perspective, the issue is clear. Religion, as described by Durkheim, has been categorized halakhically: it is *avodah zarah,* idol worship, no less evident when the idol is the society or the state than when it is a statue or a graven image. However, the public dimension of religion relates even to proper piety and worship. Even the service of God, for its own sake, recognized as an independent goal, not adulterated as a means to the achievement of the demands of an apotheosized society, is rooted in the community as well as the individual. Herein lies the duality of religion: at once a personal and a social phenomenon.

This duality stems from man's complex situation and fate. Man has a relationship to eternity and to the temporal. Therefore, two obligations and two destinies confront him. One is self–improvement, a catharsis of the soul in preparation for encountering the Divine Presence in the world of beatitude. With this thought R. Moshe Hayyim Luzzatto opens his *Mesillat Yesharim:*

> The cornerstone of piety and the root of sincere service is the resolution by every man of his duty in life…. [F]or this reason man was put in this world, so that, taking advantage of the opportunities and faculties that come his way, he may reach the place destined for him, that is, the next world.

From this perspective, man has no interest in the society that will evolve from him and his progeny. "All generations," said the historian Ranke, "stand equidistant from eternity."[61]

Man, however, has a second mission. He is not only a creation of eternity but a child of history. Judaism specifically stressed this destiny. Greek philosophy, in general, minimized the importance of history. For Plato and his school, this world is nothing more than a meager shadow, a reflection of an image of the world of ideas which alone have true metaphysical permanence. To the Stoics, the annals of history are merely a repetitive cycle, barren of innovation. In contrast, Judaism insists that history is decisively important, its events effecting major changes, generating real turning points. For Judaism, history is a process with a beginning and end, spanning "world to world," from the specific moment of initial creation until the realization of the vision in which "God will be one and His Name one." Such a relationship mandates that man, who finds himself in the framework of history, bears an obligation toward it. However, every effort to discharge this obligation removes man from his domain of privacy, for the process of history is, by its very nature, collective. Therefore, insofar as religion seeks to hasten eschatological fulfillment directly—and how can it shirk such a responsibility?—it must necessarily infiltrate the life of the community.[62] From this perspective, society is not seen merely as an avenue or backdrop to the attainment of individual spiritual values. The group's life and progress are transformed into a field of operations for the individual, and into one of his destinies. "It is not incumbent upon him to finish the work," but the task is, nonetheless, his.

This duality—of private and communal life concomitantly, of simultaneous attachment to eternity and the temporal—is reflected in every person's life. We can, however, find an especially salient example in the lives of humanity's elect—the prophets. Who can match the prophet in striving for superior sanctity? Who, as much as he, yearns to be alone with his Maker? Who, like him, is lonely, "consecrating himself, separating himself from the popular course followed in darkness?"[63] Who, more than the prophet, is preoccupied with self-creation? "And when the spirit descends upon him, his soul mingles in the upper spheres of the angels called Ishim, and he is transformed into a different person, aware that he is no longer as he was, but, rather, elevated above all wise human beings, as is said to Saul:[64] 'and you will prophesy with them and become a different person.' "[65]

Is the prophet, then, detached from reality, indifferent to the course of human events? Not at all. On the contrary, Scripture portrays the prophet primarily as a fighter, a leader, as one who is concerned for his nation's fate and character. The flame that burns in his heart, shut up in his bones, turns into a fire that consumes wickedness, purifying the world. Again, who can match the prophet in becoming a partner to the Almighty not only in the act of Creation, but also in the fashioning of generations, in molding history as in shaping nature? But this activity forces him to abandon his solitude and join the life of his generation. God, claim the kabbalists, created the world by *tzimtzum*–withdrawal; man, on the contrary, can become God's partner in creation only through expansion.[66]

To this point, we have dealt with the duality of religious life in its universal context. However, in a Jewish context, the problem is even more acute. *Knesset Yisrael* is not merely a sociopolitical setting in which every individual strives to pave his own path to *Ha–Kadosh Barukh Hu*. Nor is it an embellished means, or fertile field, for the prodding of universal human history. It is defined as "a kingdom of priests and a holy nation,"[67] its whole being and autonomy depending upon its character as a people serving God. And we may underscore nation–not a chorus of individuals or an assembly of persons–but a nation: the people in its entirety.

In Halakhah, this point is emphasized in several spheres. Most important, of course, is the dictum that "all Israel are responsible for one other."[68] But the notion is reflected–and perhaps more noticeably–in other areas. Thus, the Ramban states that if *K'lal Yisrael* were to congregate at a specified time to bring a sacrifice in partnership, the sacrifice would not be a *korban tzibbur*, a public offering of all Israel, but a sacrifice of partners, for here they do not appear as a unitary group but as an assemblage of individuals.[69] Moreover, the character of full–fledged *tzibbur* is such that it transcends the confines of time and space. A later generation, suggests Rav Papa, may offer a bull for a transgression through ignorance (*par he'alem davar*) of an earlier generation, even if not one member of the generation that perpetrated the sin is still alive, "for there is no death for the *tzibbur*."[70] The Congregation of Israel, from the revelation at Sinai until the millennium, constitutes a single organic unit–at once metaphysical and social, if you will–that is destined to be "holy to the Lord, the first fruits of His produce."[71] "Not with our ancestors did God forge this covenant, but with us, today, here, all of us alive."[72] Not with our ancestors alone, adds Rashi.[73] For as much as the individual is embedded in *K'lal Yisrael* and does not just float upon it, the communal element assumes a significant role in his spiritual life, based both on the character of the nation and on his drawing closer to its future. This fact intensifies the duality in the life of the Jew.

Hence, the tension of the dialectic inherent in *gerut* is sharpened even further. A real gap exists between, for example, *gerut* and the parallel term "conversion," as understood by many Gentile scholars. Christian discussions describe a phenomenon totally different from the Jewish conception. In the most famous of these descriptions, two chapters devoted to the subject by William James in his *The Varieties of Religious Experience*,[74] we read page after page of delicate and sensitive analysis, yet sense that the subject is not *gerut* at all, but the psychology of *teshuvah*, repentance. Since, in fact, James promises a religion with pretensions to universality, there is no significant *religious* place for entry into a congregation or community; hence, there is hardly a difference between repentance and conversion. In Jewish *gerut, le–havdil*, the communal point is fundamental. For the *ger,* his day of entry into the covenant is, as for the whole nation at Sinai, "a day of Assembly."[75]

And so, I conclude with that with which I began: the problematic. We may not ignore the duality, even the antinomy, in *gerut.* It is not ours to resolve the issue, but to clarify it. We shall overcome it only insofar as we recognize it–being sensitive to it on the practical level, and pondering it on the theoretical plane; if we fuse empathy with elucidation. It is not for us to choose between the two factors, nor do we desire to do so–God forbid. Both are essential, but our obligation is to understand and balance their relationship. The tension within *gerut* exists, but, acknowledging its existence, we may be able to master it. When the *ger* grasps the scope and the complexity of his commitment, and the members of the *bet din* are attentively attuned to the possible stirrings of his heart, then, out of their mutual sensitivity to the majesty and the tones of the event, the gap will be bridged.

Proper understanding will only issue, however, if we place the matter in the proper framework: the duality in *gerut* is indispensable and dialectical. It is inherent in the nature of religious life in general both, in its universal form and, principally, within the structure of *Knesset Yisrael.* The dialectic that exists between the individual and the community in religious life is reflected in the duality of the *gerut* process, in which the two separate factors meet in mutual relationship. Insofar as a conflict exists between them, it does not stem from the blurring of terms and experiences, but is the result of the richness of Jewish life, with all its fertile consequences and variegated nature. The gate matches the home.

Notes

1. Shemot 22:20; compare ibid. 23:9 and Vayikra 19:33.
2. Bava Metzia 59b. See also the Rambam's *Sefer Ha–Mizvot,* the beginning of the ninth shoresh (in Rav Heller's edition, pp. 19–20), in which he explains, in light of his opinion of multiple warnings for one commandment, that the transgressor does not violate three actual negative commandments, but only one, which is merely "strengthened" by the repetition of the admonitions. But in the Mishneh Torah, *Hilkhot Mekhirah* 14:15–17, the Rambam sets down that one does literally transgress three negative commandments. However, his words there require further explanation in their own right, for it appears that in reference to a *ger* he ruled that all who vex the *ger* either verbally or financially violate both *issurim,* whereas for vexing a Jew he made a distinction between the two. See also the problem raised by the discussion in the gemara, ad loc. The commentators on the Mishneh Torah deal with this at length.
3. See Bava Metzia 59b and the sources cited in the notes of Rav Hayyim Heller on the *Sefer Ha–Mizvot,* loc. cit.
4. 1 Melakhim 18:21.
5. Arthur Darby Nock, *Conversion* (Oxford, 1933), p. 12.
6. Bereshit 21:27.
7. My approach here is phenomenological, and I am dealing with types. From a sociological standpoint, the issue must be dealt with quite differently, but the two approaches are not mutually exclusive.
8. Tehillim 119:19.
9. Mekhilta de–Rabbi Yishmael, *Mishpat*im, portion 18; in the Horowitz–Rabin edition, p. 312.
10. Tehillim 42:2. I quote the verse in light of the explanation of the words in the Targ: די מרגג, "that desires." The Septuagint translates likewise, and from there the Vulgate, *desiderat.* But Rashi

accepted the interpretation of Dunash that the verb refers to the ram's cry; the *Midrash Shoher Tov,* following in the same vein, understood the whole psalm as placed in a time of exile and calamity.

11. Tehillim 63:2.

12. *Hilkhot Issurei Bi'ah* 13:4. His three–way division is of fundamental importance, but this is not the place to analyze it.

13. Yevamot 22a.

14. On genealogy, see Yevamot 22a and 97b; on inheritance, Kiddushin 17b; and concerning reproduction, Yevamot 62a. In the same vein, Rabbi Yohanan and Resh Lakish disagreed about whether the firstborn son of a *ger* born after his father's conversion is considered the firstborn for inheritance. Similarly, the halakhah is cited with respect to the acquittal of the *ger* for all his transgressions prior to his conversion; see Yevamot 48b and Sanhedrin 71b. The breadth of the halakhah as regards genealogy depends upon a dispute among the Rishonim as to whether a son of a *giyoret* (female proselyte), conceived and born after the conversion, is forbidden from marrying his mother's daughter, born prior to the mother's conversion, who herself converted before the son's birth. Rashi is of the opinion that it is only forbidden by rabbinic injunction, since by Torah law he has no attachment to a daughter born as a non–Jew. However, Rabbenu David forbids it even according to the Torah, evidently assuming that *gerut* severs all relationships that exist at the time of the *gerut,* but does not totally discard the attachment of the *ger* to his family. See *Hiddushei Ha–Ran* on Sanhedrin 58a. s.v. *ger.*

15. *Tosefta* Horayot 2:7.

16. Va–ethanan, piska 32.

17. Portion 39:14; in the Theodor–Albeck edition, p. 379.

18. Hilkhot Teshuvah 2:4.

19. Yevamot 46b.

20. Ibid.

21. Hilkhot Issurei Bi'ah 13:6. The simplest understanding of the talmudic passage in Yevamot 46b bases the prohibition against immersion on Sabbath and holidays upon *tikkunei gavra,* improving the state of a person, similar to the prohibition against sprinkling water on the ritually unclean on Sabbaths and holidays (see Pesahim 65b). Apparently, it has no juridical basis. But the Rambam, perhaps because he understood that the gemara reversed itself at the end of its discussion, related *tevilah* back to juridical roots.

22. See *Hiddushei Ha–Ramban* on Yevamot 46b, where he deliberates the point but ultimately concludes that a second *tevilah* is required by day.

23. See Yevamot 104a and Sanhedrin 34b.

24. Hilkhot lssurei Bi'ah 13:7.

25. See Yevamot 45b, Tosafot, s.v. *mi.* According to their understanding of the text, that the *tevilah* of menstruants serves as the model for the *tevilah* of *gerim,* some basis for this opinion can be found in it. However, the Rambam understood that the *tevilah* of menstruants is nothing more than an indicator that the entire procedure of *gerut* has already taken place, as implied by his mentioning other indications as well ("a *giyoret* who has been seen practicing Jewish customs consistently," e.g., she immerses herself after her menstrual cycle she separates *terumah* from her dough, etc.; see Hilkhot Issurei Bi'ah 13:9); and according to this, the talmudic reference proves nothing.

26. Kiddushin 62b, Tosafot, s.v. *ger.* Rav Yizhak Alfasi (the Rif) on Yevamot 45b likewise distinguishes between *le–khat'hila* (the proper way of performing a commandment) and *di–avad.* In the opinion of the Tur (Yoreh De'ah 268), if one immersed in the presence of two judges, married a Jewish woman, and had a son, then the son would be a Jew, for the father's immersion was acceptable *di–avad.* According to this, the Rif's position corresponds to the opinion of Tosafot, and it was indeed interpreted as such by the *Shiltei Ha–Gibborim,* ad loc. However, close analysis of the Rif's wording indicates, *prima facie,* that he is discussing whether a different *gerut* had been performed prior to this one; he does not deal with *bet din* as validating the act of *gerut* in this *tevilah.* If so, then his opinion corresponds to that of the Rambam, who presumably based himself upon the Rif. See the *Bah,* sec. 268, who argues convincingly in this vein.

27. On these two sides of *gerut,* see the work of my master, Rav J.B. Soloveitchik, *Kol Dodi Dofek,* in *Ish Ha–Emunah* (Jerusalem 1968), pp. 95–99, especially the footnotes. The Rav sees the two

aspects of conversion as embodied in the two covenants that evolved from two historical events, the Exodus from Egypt and the Revelation at Sinai. The major thrust of this article is based on the essential cornerstone laid down in that work, but I will not go into the stages of *gerut* here.

A different interpretation of the character of circumcision and *tevilah* was suggested by Rav Yosef Engel in the *Gilyonei Ha-Shas,* Yevamot 46a. Compare also the *Milhamot Hashem* of the Ramban, Shabbat 135a.

28. Hilkhot lssurei Bi'ah 14:1.

29. Yevamot 47a.

30. Hilkhot Teshuvah 3:11. However, Rashi to Sanhedrin 47a, s.v. *mi–darkhei tzibbur,* explains, "such as an apostate." On the connection of the Rambam to this topic, see *Kol Dodi Dofek,* p. 96.

31. Bikkurim 1:4.

32. Ibid. But the *Tosefta* reads (Bikkurim 1:2): "Rabbi Yehudah says: All the *gerim* bring the first fruits but do not utter the declaration; the sons of Keni, Mosheh's father–in–law, bring the first fruits and utter the declaration." The issue was discussed by the Rishonim; see the sources cited in *Tosefta Ki–Peshutah* by Rabbi Saul Lieberman, pp. 823–825.

33. Hilkhot Bikkurim 4:3, 34. In his *hiddushim* to Bava Batra 81a.

35. Yeshayahu 56:3. The text reads, however, "shall surely separate me."

36. The Rambam's Responsa, Blau edition, no. 293; 11:549. It is worth noting that according to his view, there may, *prima facie*, be a halakhic ramification. A *ger toshav* may trace himself to Avraham (and if we presume, as did the Ramban, loc. cit., that "the three patriarchs of the world were like Avraham," then he may trace himself to Yizhak and Yaakov as well), but he may not say "who took us out of Egypt."

37. Sukkah 49b.

38. See above, n. 6.

39. Sanhedrin 93a.

40. Bereshit Rabbah 42:13; in the Theodor–Albeck edition. p. 414.

41. Bereshit 17:9.

42. Lekh Lekha: Buber edition, p. 31.

43. Devarim 9:10.

44. Yeshayahu 26:2.

45. Ruth 1:16.

46. Ruth 2:11–12. Despite this emphasis, we need not be surprised that Ruth described and perhaps perceived herself as an alien (*nokhriyyah*). Even if we discount the possible explanation that the words apply only to her roots, and not to her present state, we may intuit that although she desired to identify with *Knesset Yisrael,* her social–personal integration was still incomplete. However, the famous description of Keats, who ruminates that the nightingale's is "Perhaps the self–same song that found a path / Through the sad heart of Ruth, when sick, for home, / She stood in tears amid the alien corn" (*Ode to a Nightingale,* vv, 65–67) is purely conjectural and has no basis in the text.

47. Needless to say, in the preceding section I do not mean to suggest that changes occurred in the laws of *gerut,* but refer to changes in the atmosphere surrounding it, with varying emphases in specific cases and perhaps in specific periods.

48. Yevamot 46b. Rabbi Yehoshua holds that *tevilah* without *milah* is sufficient, *post facto*, for *gerut.*

49. Hilkhot Issurei Bi'ah 14:2. In the gemara (Yevamot 47a), only a description of the *mizvot* is mentioned. Presumably, theological rudiments were to be discussed during the course of the exposition; nevertheless, the Rambam's express reference is noteworthy.

50. Hilkhot Issurei Bi'ah 14:6; based on Yevamot 47b.

51. See Niddah 28a, Berakhot 46b,

52. Hilkhot Issurei Bi'ah 10:6. He refers there to a live fetus; with respect to a miscarriage, to exempt the child who follows from the title of firstborn, the Rambam required the whole forehead (Hilkhot Bekhorim 11:15). In the former case, the law of birth takes effect through the emergence of the head in its own right; hence, even most of the forehead, which is considered most of the head, is sufficient. In the latter case, since there is no person, the head is considered nothing more than the representative of most of the body, and most of the head no longer suffices (from Rav J.B. Soloveitchik).

53. Shir Ha–Shirim 4:12.

54. On the basis of his experience in dealing with *gerim*. Rabbi Zeʹev Gotthold has pointed out to me that many of them, facing a very confusing transitional period in their lives, derive spiritual support from the presence of the *bet din*. In his opinion, most *gerim* view it as supportive rather than as interference. Yet perhaps, ideally speaking, the contradiction persists, and I am inclined to assume that it is a factor in many specific instances.

55. See the opinion of Rabbi Netanel in the Tosafot, Kiddushin 62b, s.v. *ger,* and in the *Hiddushei Ha–Ramban* on Yevamot 46b. It should be pointed out that the term "laymen" in this context has a specific halakhic sense, referring to persons who have not been formally or technically ordained, and is not to be understood in its usual sense.

56. See above, n. 24.

57. *Enneads* 6:9.

58. Alfred North Whitehead, *Religion in the Making* (New York, 1927), p. 17.

59. See Émile Durkheim, *Les formes élémentaires de la vie religieuse* (Paris, 1912), passim.

60. See Bronistlaw Malinowski, *Magic, Science and Religion* (Garden City, NY, 1948), esp. pp. 54–60.

61. Quoted in Herbert Butterfield, *Christianity and History* (London, 1957), p. 89.

62. Of course, we may indirectly bring *ge'ulah* closer by serving God in the strictly private domain, for this brings in its wake an increase in divine assistance.

63. Hilkhot Yesodei ha–Torah 7:1.

64. I Shemuel 10:6.

65. Rambam, loc. cit.

66. From time to time, the prophet requires withdrawal in order to prepare himself for prophecy. But the fulfillment of his task necessarily demands expansion.

67. Shemot 19:6.

68. Shevuot 39a.

69. *Milhamot Hashem,* Berakhot, chap. 3. In his commentary on the Torah (Vayikra 1:2) he assumes that this is Rashi's opinion, but there, he himself leans toward assuming that "if the *tzibbur* desires to set aside funds for a voluntary sacrifice, and money is raised [for that purpose] as *shekalim* are similarly collected for daily and additional sacrifices, then this would be a *nidvat tzibbur.*"

70. Horayot 6a. After some discussion, the gemara reaches the conclusion that there is no source for this law and it is likely that one generation cannot atone for another unless some members of the earlier generation are still alive. This notwithstanding, the notion of a link between generations remains valid. Even according to the conclusion, it is not the individual persons remaining who sacrifice the atonement, but the whole *tzibbur.* The need for a remnant is just a stipulation required of a sacrifice for a transgression that there be present "offerers" who have a direct connection to the offering. In any case, the position that "there is no death in the *tzibbur*" has been already established. Thus, the Halakhah pertaining to a *hattat* (sin–offering) whose owners have died," i.e., that it cannot be offered or redeemed but must graze until it dies, does not apply to a *hattat tzibbur,* as its "owner" never dies. See Rambam, Hilkhot Pesulei ha–Mukdashim 4:1.

71. Yirmiyahu 2:3.

72. Devarim 5:3.

73. Ibid.; see the two interpretations of Ibn Ezra ad loc.

74. See William James, *The Varieties of Religious Experience* (New York, 1902), chaps. 9–10. A similar bent is evident in some of those who followed James: e.g., A.C. Underwood, *Conversion: Christian and Non–Christian* (New York, 1925); W. Bryn Thomas, *The Psychology of Conversion* (London, 1935); Robert O. Ferm, *The Psychology of Christian Conversion* (Westwood, NY, 1959). To a degree, this notion is incorporated into a general emphasis on the subjective that is an outgrowth of dealing with the psychological side of the issue, and that is noticeable, in particular, among Protestant authors. However, it exists even among those whose bent lends more importance to the formal, objective points. e.g., Catholics. In a different sense, it is essential to Catholics even more than to Protestants, since universalism is at the core of Catholic theology.

75. The concept of a religious *tzibbur* as a distinct social, organic unit is not, of course, foreign to Christianity, and it served from its inception as one of the fundamental points in the formative molding of the Church as idea and institution. Moreover, another central dimension was added during the Protestant Reformation, as national churches evolved, at which time the concept actu-

ally served as a major bone of contention, especially in England. But this concept never paralleled that of *Knesset Yisrael*, even during the Reformation. In the writings of the Anglican divine Richard Hooker (*Laws of Ecclesiastical Polity*, book 8), the idea of an *ecclesia* was, in essence, universal, and he sought primarily to search and find, within this framework, room for a national entity, despite its being, relatively speaking, an artificial unit.

On the other hand, in earlier societies, the interweaving of religion and nation, or of religion and city–state, was the norm, both encompassing the same group. But this is effective only in a polytheistic framework, wherein the idol and its worship were limited to a specific place and community, and bears no similarity whatsoever to our conception, which, in comparison with polytheism, is thoroughly universal.

THE CONVERSION CRISIS: A HALAKHIC ANALYSIS
J. David Bleich

"1 am the one who drew Yitro nigh and did not repulse him. You, also, when a person comes to you to be converted AND COMES SOLELY FOR THE SAKE OF HEAVEN draw him nigh and do not repulse him."

YALKUT SHIM'ONI, YITRO, 268

Jew today, no less than in the past, is the heir to an unbroken chain of tradition. Survival of the Jew is directly dependent upon preservation of the divinely sanctified identity of the community of Israel. The sanctity of Israel is a concomitant of Israel's acceptance of the Torah on Mount Sinai, a Torah which is an inseparable whole comprised of both Holy Writ and the Oral Law. Thus, for Judaism itself, the question "Who is a Jew?" can have but one answer: A Jew is one whom Halakhah defines as a Jew.

Jews, jealous of their identity, have always heroically resisted any and all attempts to compromise their ethic purity. As the Midrash queries, "Why did Jeremiah compare Israel to the olive? All liquids intermingle with one another; oil is immiscible, and remains apart. Similarly, Israel cannot be assimilated among the nations of the world,"[1] Our survival as a people may undoubtedly be credited to our tenacity in preserving inviolate the identity of the Jew.

Yet the peoplehood of Israel is not founded upon racist attitudes nor has Judaism suffered from the maladies of xenophobia. Jewish identity has always been a matter of membership in a specific and unique faith–community. As such Judaism has always welcomed all individuals seeking to embrace the tenets of the Torah. Indeed, the *ger zedek* (righteous proselyte) is extolled in Rabbinic literature and depicted as being the recipient of an extraordinary degree of Divine favor. The *ger zedek* is regarded with awe and wonder. Whereas the Jews who experienced the giving of the Torah at Mount Sinai were so overwhelmed by the difficulties attendant upon the observance of the commandments that they had to be coerced in order to secure their acceptance of the precepts of the Torah, the proselyte voluntarily accepts this discipline. "Had they not witnessed the sounds and the flames, the thunder and the voice of the *shofrot* they would not have accepted the yoke of the kingdom of heaven. Yet this (convert) did not witness a single one of these and joins himself to the Lord and accepts the yoke of the kingdom of heaven. Can there be anyone more beloved!"[2] The delight which God takes in such converts is reflected in the explicit halakhic obligation making it incumbent upon the rabbinical courts to accept sincere and committed candidates for proselytization.

However, in the demands which it makes upon the proselyte Judaism is uncompromising, Judaism is not merely a faith community; its adherents are bound by a rigorous and demanding code of law governing every aspect of life. Commitment must be total. To be accepted as a member of the community of Israel the convert must not only subscribe to the beliefs of Judaism but must willingly agree to observe its precepts. Should the candidate refuse to accept any detail of this code, his conversion is *ipso facto* invalid.

In this Judaism is unyielding. The basic conditions of genuine conversion are clearly enunciated in Halakhah. As the guardians of a Divine mandate Jews must perforce refuse to recognize any conversion not performed in accordance with the norms of Halakhah. This stark reality cannot be altered by the fiat of any civil judicial body. Nor for that matter is any rabbinic court or other ecclesiastic body empowered to overlook the *sina qua non* of Jewish identity.

Present circumstances have added a new dimension to the "Who is a Jew?" problem. The high incidence of intermarriage both in Israel and the Diaspora has generated an unprecedented number of applications for conversion. Given the exigencies of the contemporary situation conversion may well be the solution to marred personal, social and religious problems. On the other hand, improper procedure may not only reduce the conversion ritual to a meaningless charade but may also pose a threat to the very identity of the Jewish people.

The responsa literature of the modern period is replete with questions concerning the circumstances under which conversion is permissible and proper. These discussions are clearly germane to any attempt to find a resolution to the current conversion dilemma. The questions posed with regard to problematic contemporary conversions are threefold in nature: (1) Is it permissible for rabbinical courts to accept prospective candidates for conversion when it appears that application is made, not out of religious conviction, but as a matter of convenience, e.g., to facilitate marriage with a Jewish partner? (2) Is a conversion of convenience, *i.e.*, one undertaken for marriage or other ulterior motive in which the petitioner obviously has no intention of abiding by the precepts of Judaism, a valid one? (3) Granting the validity and propriety of the conversion itself, is it permissible for the convert to enter into marriage with a Jewish spouse with whom the convert has consorted prior to conversion?

I

The Gemara (*Yevamot* 24b) cites the opinion of R. Nechemiah who maintained that any conversion based upon ulterior motivation is null and void. In addition to conversion for purposes of marriage, R. Nechemiah specifically refers to the recorded historical episodes of the conversion of the Samaritans predicated upon fear of lions,[3] conversion by servants of King Solomon in anticipation of being appointed to high office in the royal court, and the mass conversions which are recorded in the Book of Esther[4] as instances of invalid conversion. The Gemara rejects the opinion of R. Nechemiah as applied to conversions which are already a *fait accompli*.[5] Once performed, such conversions are valid regardless of motivation. Nevertheless, Jewish law is unequivocal in stating that before the fact such candidates are not to be accepted. The *Bet Din* is constrained to reject applicants prompted by motives other than sincere religious conviction. Thus, *Hagahot Mordekhai. Yevamot*, sec. 110, writes that if it is known that the applicants are motivated by desire of personal benefit "they are not be accepted." Moreover, the Gemara flatly declares that proselytes will not be accepted in the days of the Messiah and in fact, were not accepted during the reigns of David and Solomon. The reason for blanket rejection of would–be converts during these historical epochs is that in periods during which the Jewish commonwealth is blessed with economic prosperity and prestigious social status there is ample room for suspicion that prospective proselytes are not prompted by reasons of sincere religious conviction.

Rambam,[6] in his codification of these regulations, is even more explicit:

> Let it not enter your mind that Samson, the deliverer of Israel, or Solomon, king of Israel, who was called "beloved of God," married foreign women while they were yet gentiles, but rather the secret of the matter is as follows: The proper performance of the precept is that when a male or female proselyte comes to be converted, he is to be investigated[7] perchance he seeks to enter the [Jewish] religion in order to acquire money or in order to achieve a position of authority or because of fear. In the case of a man, he is to be investigated perchance he has set his eyes upon a Jewish woman; in the case of a woman, [she] is to be investigated perchance she set her eyes upon one of the youths of Israel. If no motive is found in them, the heavy weight of the yoke of the Torah is to be made known to them and the burden which there is for gentiles in its observance. Therefore, the *Bet Din* did not accept proselytes throughout the days of David and Solomon. In the days of David, lest they rejected [idol worship] because of fear and in the days of Solomon, lest they rejected [idol worship] because of the sovereignty, the prosperity and the greatness which Israel then enjoyed. For whosoever forsakes heathenism for the sake of some worldly vanity is not a righteous proselyte. Nevertheless, many proselytes were converted in the days of David and Solomon by ignorant persons and the Great Court accorded them doubtful status, not rejecting them . . and not drawing them nigh until such time as their subsequent conduct could be observed.

It is quite evident that prospective converts are to be rejected even if proof positive of ulterior motive is lacking. The mere suspicion of impure motive is grounds for rejection of the applicant's candidacy; the burden of proof with regard to sincerity is upon the prospective convert.[8] Apparently, when it is obvious that material benefit or personal gain would accrue to the proselyte, protestations of religious conviction are unacceptable.

There is, however, one exception to this principle. The Gemara records several instances of converts who were accepted despite self–avowed ulterior motivation. In *Shabbat* 31a it is reported that Hillel accepted a proselyte who approached him with the declaration, "Convert me in order that you may appoint me High Priest." Similarly, *Menachot* 44a reports that R. Chiya accepted the candidacy of a woman who wished to convert in order to become the wife of one of his students. *Tosafot, Yevamot* 24b, resolves the apparent incongruity by postulating that Hillel and R. Chiya were certain that the respective candidates would ultimately accept Judaism "for the sake of heaven."[9] All authorities agree that an application for conversion may justifiably be entertained only if the *Bet Din* is satisfied that upon conversion the candidate will become a God–fearing Jew and will scrupulously observe the commandments of the Torah. It is clear that, according to Halakhah, certainty of future religious observance is a necessary condition for acceptance of a prospective convert.

In a letter written in response to a question submitted on behalf of the Sephardic community of Buenos Aires, Rabbi Meshullam Roth[10] declares that the candidacy of a prospective proselyte cannot under any circumstances be considered unless the candidate assures the *Bet Din* that he will observe the precepts of Judaism, particularly the laws of the Sabbath, family purity and the dietary code. If, in the opinion of the *Bet Din* it is "virtually certain" that he will fulfill his pledge and the *Bet Din* feels that ultimately the conversion will be "for the sake of heaven," they may then perform the conversion ritual. Rabbi Roth notes, however, that the percentage of convert whose intention is for the "sake of heaven" is so minute that in actuality it "approaches zero."

Some authorities grant considerable leeway in determining sincerity of purpose. R. Shlomo Kluger[11] discusses the propriety of sanctioning the conversion of a young man who threatened to become an apostate if his non–Jewish mistress would not be accepted as a proselyte. Rabbi Kluger rules that under such circumstances the conversion cannot be considered as having been undertaken on account of marriage, since the couple will continue to live together as man and wife in any event. Hence, the conversion may be deemed to be "for the sake of heaven" and not "for the sake of man." A similar view was voiced by R. Eliezer Deutsch and by R. Yechiel Yaakov Weinberg.[12] This contention is also cited by R. Chaim Ozer Grodzinski,[13] and applied by him to the case of a couple who had undergone a civil ceremony and were living together as man and wife. This opinion is, however, by no means universally accepted. R. Meir Arak[14] rejects this view arguing that ulterior motivation is indeed present in that the husband may well wish to legitimize his marriage and not continue an illicit relationship. There is evidence that R. Chaim Ozer himself later reversed his position with regard to this matter and adopted a more stringent attitude. In a responsum dealing with a similar problem dated some twenty–two years later and published in Vol. III, no. 28, of the same work, *Teshuvot Achiezer*, R. Chaim Ozer regards conversion under similar circumstances as being undertaken for the sake of marriage and, hence, prohibits it. Even though the couple were not only living together as man and wife but had also sired children without having contracted a valid marriage, R. Chaim Ozer rules that the prospective proselyte was, even in this instance, motivated by reasons of marriage. The dim view expressed by these authorities regarding the permissibility of conversion despite an already existent conjugal relationship merely echoes in greater detail the succinct but unequivocal decision of a much earlier authority, R. Yaakov Ettlinger.[15]

An argument frequently advanced in favor of the acceptance of converts, regardless of motivation, is that their rejection by an Orthodox *Bet Din* is often followed by acceptance into the Jewish faith by Reform or liberal clergymen. Conversions conducted under such auspices are clearly invalid. As a result individuals converted in this manner are inadvertently accepted by the Jewish community as *bona fide* Jews and are unlawfully permitted to contract marriages with other Jews. If the alleged convert is a female, children born to her are, of course, not Jewish; if a male, the children, while Jewish, are of tainted lineage. Rabbi Mendel Kirshbaum,[16] who served as Dayan in Frankfort, argues that in light of this consideration such candidates should be accepted for conversion. The Gemara (*Yevamot* 47a) states that a prospective proselyte is to be investigated with regard to his motives for conversion and is to be informed of selected *mitzvot* of both lesser and greater stringency and of the punishments incurred upon their transgression. "For what reason?" queries the Gemara. "So that if he changes his mind, let him change his mind." Rashi, in his commentary on this text adds, "For if he should change his mind [and decide] not to convert, let him change his mind *and it is of no concern to us.*" Rabbi Kirshbaum contends that one may infer from this comment that if the conversion were to be of concern to Jewry no attempt at discouragement should be made. In instances in which considerations such as those previously stated are operative encouragement of conversion is indeed a matter of positive concern to us. Consequently, argues Rabbi Kirshbaum, under these circumstances the convert should be accepted, even if his decision to seek conversion is prompted by impure motives.[17] This contention was rejected by the late R. Yaakov Mordecai Breish of Zurich in a letter written to Rabbi Kirshbaum upon the publication of *Menachem Meshiv.*[18] Rabbi Breish states that the consideration raised is a specious one and that there need be no fear that the candidate will be erroneously accepted as a Jew. In the course of the usual investigation before any prospective marriage it should become clear that the conversion was performed by a Reform rabbi and hence is invalid. Furthermore, adds Rabbi Breish, it is forbidden for the members of the *Bet Din* to participate in a conversion for the sake of marriage and this prohibition devolves directly upon the rabbis involved. Accordingly, they are forbidden to commit this transgression even in order to prevent a more severe transgression on the part of others.[19]

II

There is strong reason to question the validity of conversion, even as a *fait accompli,* when undertaken for purposes of marriage or, for that matter, in order to obtain benefits accruing to Jews granted Israeli citizenship under the Law of Return. As previously noted, the definitive rule of the Talmud is that conversions once performed are valid even if entered into for reasons other than religious conviction. In analyzing the rationale governing the validity of sincere conversions, the most obvious reason which presents itself is the Halakhic principal that mental reservations cannot invalidate an overt act –*devarim she–be–lev ainam devarim.* Hence, even if the act were to be mentally nullified, the conversion would be efficacious. Accordingly, the conversion cannot be invalidated by reservations or insincere motives which remain in *pectore*. However, a quite different line of reasoning explaining the validity of such conversion is presented by the Ritva and Nemukei Yosef in their commentaries on *Yevamot* 24b. These authorities state that all conversions stemming from ulterior motivation are not merely lacking in sincerity, but in a sense, are not undertaken in free will and embody an element of coercion. Nevertheless, conversion as a *fait accompli* is valid even under these circumstances because such coercion ultimately engenders a firm decision to accept the obligations attendant upon acceptance of Judaism. The candidate for conversion recognizes that his desired goal can be achieved only by making such a commitment and accordingly accepts the obligations incumbent upon a member of the Jewish faith. Since Ritva and Nemukei Yosef are intent upon disspelling the notion that mental reservations exist in instances of insincere conversion we must infer that mental reservations, when and if they are present, would, according to these authorities, invalidate the conversion. The ramifications of this crucial issue are discussed by R. Isaac Schmelkes. In his *Bet Yitzchak*,[20] he explains that mental reservations do serve to invalidate conversion because, in his opinion, the general principle that mental negations are ineffective applies only with regard to matters affecting interpersonal relationships such as financial transactions and the like. Matters such as conversion are essentially ritual in nature and "the Lord desires the heart." Hence, it is the ultimate intention which prevails. The Talmud[21] states that a non–Jew who refuses to accept even a single commandment or a single Rabbinic ordinance, must be rejected, since such non–acceptance invalidates conversion. Accordingly, argues *Bet Yitzchak*, converts who have reservations with regard to the acceptance of the dietary laws and laws of family purity cannot be regarded as Jews even if they falsely declare that they are willing to fulfill all the precepts of Judaism. Rabbi Schmelkes declares that such conversions should not be performed not only because the conversions are themselves farcical in nature but also because they leave in their wake spurious proselytes who are commonly accepted as Jews. These invalid conversions subsequently lead to unions between Jews and individuals who are gentiles in the eyes of Halakhah.

R. Chaim Ozer Grodzenski[22] agrees that mental reservations with regard to performance of *mitzvot* nullify the efficacy of ritual conversion. He cites as evidence for this position the terminology of Rambam:

> A convert who has not been investigated . . . who has been circumcised and has immersed himself in the presence of three ignorant persons is a proselyte, even if it be known that he has converted on account of some consideration . . . he is accorded doubtful status until his righteousness becomes clear.[23]

The "doubtful status" of a proselyte prompted by ulterior motivation, explains R. Chaim Ozer, arises from the fact that actual conversion is ultimately a matter of intent. If the candidate does indeed accept Judaism with all its ramifications he is deemed to be a Jew regardless of motivation; but if these considerations do not ultimately lead to a wholehearted acceptance the conversion is invalid. When no extraneous considerations are present there is no reason to doubt the validity of the conversion: when such considerations are present, the status of the proselyte remains in doubt until such time as his "righteousness is demonstrated," i.e. until such time as his general comportment testifies to ultimate acceptance of the norms of Jewish conduct.[24]

An explication of the concept of mental reservation in this context is formulated by R. Chaim Ozer[25] who notes a fundamental distinction between *acceptance* of precepts and *observance* of precepts. The stipulation that a prospective convert must accept all commandments of the Torah means simply that he must accept their binding force. Recognition by the candidate that he is lacking in moral stamina or the requisite willpower to withstand temptation does not invalidate a conversion. R. Chaim Ozer adds, however, that when it is evident that the prospective convert intends to desecrate the Sabbath and to partake of forbidden foods as a matter of course the conversion is invalid. Such an attitude on the part of the candidate is indicative of non–acceptance of these prohibitions in principle and hence nullifies the act of conversion.

R. Chaim Ozer's basic distinction between acceptance and observance of precepts is challenged by the one–time Chief Rabbi of Kovno, Rabbi Abraham Dov Ber Kahane. In his collected responsa, *D'var Avraham*,[26] Rabbi Kahane contends that acceptance of the "yoke of commandments" coupled with clear intention to transgress is a self–contradiction and cannot be termed "acceptance" at all.[27] While disagreeing with regard to what may constitute mental reservations both authorities concur that when mental reservations are present, the conversion is invalid.

The necessity for the convert's acceptance of the "yoke of mitzvot" as a *sine qua non* of his conversion raises certain difficulties in our generation. As noted earlier the rationale advanced by numerous authorities in defense of the *ex post facto* validity of insincere conversions is the consideration that in such instances there is ultimately a determined, albeit reluctant, acceptance of the obligations incurred through the acceptance of Judaism. In the absence of anticipated benefit a candidate lacking deep religious commitment might not wish to incur such responsibilities. Yet weighing the pros and cons of the situation determination to accept the tenets of Judaism is reached by the convert upon recognition that only by the acceptance of such obligations will the benefits attendant upon membership in the Jewish faith–community accrue to him. It is, in a sense, a bargain in which the desire for certain benefits forces acceptance of concomitant disadvantages. Rabbi Kahane argues that a changed social and religious climate no longer demands such a decision on the part of a convert. A convert lacking sincerity of motivation is forced to accept the obligations incumbent upon members of the Jewish faith only if he lives in a society which demands that he conform to the normative standards of Jewish life. In such a milieu the desired benefits can be obtained by the convert only by accepting the tenets of Judaism. Hence, the resolution to embrace Judaism, even if motivated by self–serving considerations, constitutes a valid acceptance. In contemporary society, however, pressure for religious conformity does not exist. Consequently, declares Rabbi Kahane, nowadays in cases where a deeply–rooted commitment of faith is not the moving factor there is no reason to assume that ulterior motivation mandates even a "coerced" acceptance.

Similar misgivings concerning the status of such conversions in our day are echoed in the relatively recent writings of numerous Halakhic authorities. Particularly forceful are the strictures expressed by the late Chief Rabbi of Israel, Rabbi Isaac ha–Levi Herzog. In a letter addressed to a Swiss rabbinic body he writes:

> . . . even though the halakhic decision has been formulated that, after the fact, even those converting for ulterior purposes and not for the sake of heaven are converts, I have exceedingly strong reason [to assert] that in these times the law is not so. Since in former times virtually every Jew was forced to observe the commandments, otherwise he would have been disdained and despised as a renegade, this therefore strengthened the supposition that the gentile who comes to convert has, in truth, made a decision to observe the Sabbath, etc. . . .But in our day the situation has changed and it is [now] possible to be a leader in Israel while yet a desecrator of the Sabbath and one who partakes of *nevelah* and *terefah* in public, etc. Whereby does one arrive at the supposition that the gentile indeed decided, at least at the moment of conversion, to observe Judaism? Moreover, the vast majority and perhaps all converts of this genre do not commence to observe even the fundamentals of [the Jewish] faith...[28]

Rabbi Breish[29] voices a similar opinion and states emphatically that if it is evident that the proselyte will not adhere to the tenets of Judaism the conversion ceremony is in no way efficacious. He further adds that when conversion is preliminary to marriage to a spouse who is non–observant it may be assumed with virtual certainty that the convert will be no more scrupulous in observing the commandments of the Torah than the marriage partner who is a Jew by birth. R. Meir Arak (*Imrei Yosher*, I, no. 176), R. Menachem Panet (*Avnei Zedek*, no. 26) and R. Yitzchak Yaakov Weiss (*Minchat Yitzchak*, I, no. 122) concur with the previously discussed views of *Bet Yitzchak, Achi'ezer, Dvar Avraham*, Rabbi Breish and Rabbi Herzog. All these authorities are in agreement that when it is evident that the candidate will be non–observant the conversion is null and void despite the candidate's oral declaration of acceptance of the yoke of *mitzvot*.

It is interesting to note that R. Moses Feinstein, in a responsum dated Luban 5689 (1929), voices an identical opinion and adds:

> I do not understand the reasoning of those rabbis who err with regard to this. Even according to their opinion, what benefit do they bring to the Jewish people in their acceptance of such converts? For it is certain that the Holy One blessed be He, and the Jewish people are not happy that such converts become intermingled with Israel. According to the Law, it is certain that such (a convert) is not a proselyte at all. [30]

In a later responsum,[31] written in the United States some twentyone years later, the author, while himself rejecting their position, attempts to find a "slight justification for those rabbis who accept [such converts] in order that they not be considered inferior even to ignoramuses." Rabbi Feinstein cites the argument that mental reservations cannot invalidate a performed act. In contradistinction to previously cited authorities Rabbi Feinstein accepts this argument in principle, agreeing that this canon (*devarim she–be–lev ainam devarim*) encompasses even ritual acts such as conversion. However, he declares that it is inapplicable to the case at hand. Although mental reservations in themselves cannot invalidate the oral acceptance of the yoke of *mitzvot*, nevertheless in the case of a convert who will definitely not observe the precepts of Judaism "we are witnesses" to the fact that the oral acceptance is not sincere. We are thus confronted by a phenomenon different in kind from mere mental reservation. Whereas a private mental reservation may not invalidate the conversion, common recognition that such reservations exist elevates such reservations to the status of a public act tantamount to an open declaration annulling the acceptance of commandments. Such a declaration would clearly invalidate the conversion.

Rabbi Feinstein also advances a second consideration in defense of the validity of such conversions. Unfortunately, nowadays non–observance on the part of many of our co–religionists is so widespread that the candidate for conversion may fail to appreciate what is implied by the acceptance of religious obligations. Thus, the convert may well believe that the normative fulfillment of a religious obligation is an elective act of piety and not required of every Jew. As indicated by the Gemara (*Shabbat* 68b) ignorance of even the most fundamental observance of Judaism does not invalidate conversion if on the basis of the candidate's limited knowledge, he or she has, in fact, accepted the tenets of Judaism.

III

The vast majority of questionable conversions are performed in order to facilitate marriage with a Jewish spouse and quite often occur after a civil marriage has already taken place. However, such unions present a grave Halakhic problem. Even when the conversion itself is entered into with utmost sincerity and conviction it is questionable whether a converted Jewess may marry a Jew with whom she has consorted while still a gentile.

The Mishnah[32] declares that one who is suspected of having cohabited with a gentile woman may not marry the woman in question subsequent to her conversion. The Mishnah adds, however, that if the marriage did take place the couple are not obliged to seek a divorce. Rashi explains that this prohibition was promulgated in order to safeguard the honor and reputation of the husband since marriage under such circumstances is likely to lend credence to rumors of previous immorality. On the basis of the explanation advanced by Rashi, some authorities[33] conclude that this prohibition does not encompass instances in which the couple have been living together publicly, since in such cases previous immoral conduct is an established verity.[34] Other authorities argue that there are more cogent grounds for banning such marriage if prior immoral conduct is a matter of public knowledge. Such arguments are predicated upon an alternate explanation of the considerations upon which the prohibition is based. Rashba[35] explains that the marriage of a converted Jewess to the man with whom she is suspected of having consorted prior to her conversion is forbidden lest aspersion be cast upon the sincerity of the conversion itself. If the couple are suspected of having lived together previously their marriage subsequent to conversion will lead to suspicion that the conversion itself was insincerely contrived merely for purposes of marriage. Quite obviously, according to this line of reasoning, the prohibition is more stringent if the relationship prior to conversion was a matter of public knowledge. It is also evident that the *Tosefta* and the Palestinian Talmud both regard this prohibition as being operative even in cases of positively known prior cohabitation. Rambam regards transgression of the prohibition to be graver in nature in cases of known immorality than in cases of merely suspected cohabitation. Rambam rules that when it is known with certainty that the couple have cohabited before conversion the husband is obliged to divorce his wife, even though the Mishnah in discussing cases of merely suspected immorality rules that when the marriage is a *fait accompli* divorce is unnecessary. Rabbi Schmelkes and R. Chaim Ozer, in their previously cited responsa, both argue that there is no significant disagreement between Rashi and Rashba. Marriage under the aforementioned circumstances is forbidden for a two–fold reason: it will reflect negatively upon the husband's moral reputation and will cast a cloud of suspicion over the validity of the conversion itself. It is the thesis of Rabbi Schmelkes and R. Chaim Ozer that Rashi, in stating the first of these considerations, does not dispute the rationale of Rashba who, in offering the latter, logically extends the prohibition to instances of known cohabitation. According to this analysis, Rashi presents his own explanation solely for the purpose of explaining a parallel prohibition recorded in the same Mishnah. The Mishnah declares that the same provisions regarding subsequent marriage apply with regard to one suspected of having cohabited with a female slave before her emancipation–an instance in which Rashba's consideration is not applicable since no formal commitment with regard to the acceptance of the precepts of the Torah is necessary on the part of an emancipated slave.[37]

Several authorities find reason to draw a sharp distinction between instances of known promiscuity and cases in which conversion has been preceded by a civil marriage. Rabbi Feinstein[38] asserts that even according to Rashba's interpretation the prohibition against marriage following conversion is not applicable in cases where a civil marriage has already taken place. Since the couple have already established a permanent conjugal relationship, argues Rabbi Feinstein, there can be no grounds for the suspicion that conversion was insincerely sought merely for the sake of marriage. It would seem, however, that the numerous authorities cited in an earlier section who maintain that the desire to legitimize the relationship and to contract a marriage which is valid in the eyes of Halakhah constitute an ulterior motive disqualifying the candidacy of a prospective proselyte would also deem marriage subsequent to conversion to be forbidden, according to Rashba, on these self–same grounds. R. Yosef Sha'ul Nathanson expressly forbids the marriage of a Jew and a prospective convert despite the fact that they had been married in a civil ceremony and had sired children. Such marrages are also forbidden by R. Ya'akov Ettlinger and by R. Meir Arak. [39]

Another argument sanctioning marriage once a civil ceremony has taken place is advanced by R. Meshullam Kutner.[40] Rabbi Kutner cites authorities who maintain that if a civil ceremony has already been performed the applicable Halakhah is the ruling of the Mishnah that the husband need not divorce his wife. These authorities declare that this provision is applicable not merely in cases of marriages which are Halakhically valid but encompasses all cases where a permanent conjugal relationship has been established. This ruling is also adopted by R. Benjamin Aryeh Weiss[41] and R. David Hoffmann;[42] it is, however, specifically rejected by Rabbi Weinberg.[43] Rabbi Hoffmann qualifies his position by stating that such permission cannot be granted if the rabbi was consulted prior to the civil ceremony and the candidate was rejected as being insincere in motivation. Rabbi Hoffmann further indicates that if, in practice, this lenient decision will lead to a higher incidence of intermarriage no such candidate should be accepted for conversion. In another responsum[44] Rabbi Hoffmann further circumscribes his ruling by stating that such candidates cannot be accepted unless they pledge "on their word of honor" to observe all the tenets of Judaism and specifically "the commandments concerning the Sabbath, *niddah* and forbidden foods."

There is yet another argument which may be advanced in favor of countenancing such marriages. In the vast majority of such cases the couple will continue living together as man and wife whether or not conversion and subsequent marriage will receive ecclesiastic sanction. R. Chaim of Zanz[45] raises the question of whether conversion should not be permitted and the marriage tolerated in order to spare the husband from the graver prohibition against consorting publicly with a non–Jewess. The latter transgression is clearly Biblical in nature, whereas the prohibition against marriage in this instance is of rabbinic origin. Some authorities argue that in such cases marriage following conversion should be sanctioned as constituting the lesser of two evils. R. Menachem Panet[46] permits such marriages following conversion when it is evident that the couple will, in any event, continue to live together as man and wife.

Employing a similar argument R. Shlomo Kluger ruled that the marriage may take place in the previously noted case of a young man who threatened apostasy if not permitted to marry his gentile mistress. *Achi'ezer*[47] cites a responsum of Rambam[48] in which the author sanctioned the emancipation of a slave and her subsequent marriage to a young man who was suspected of having had illicit relations with her on the grounds that, although objectively speaking this course of action is not permissible, it constitutes the lesser of two evils. The marriage is an infraction of lesser severity than continued illicit relations with a slave. *Achi'ezer* notes, however, that applied to the case at hand this argument is specious if, as is often the case, the couple have no intention of observing the laws of family purity. Apart from violation of the ban against subsequent marriage, valid conversion will cause a Biblical prohibition of *niddah* to devolve upon each act of cohabitation–a prohibition which does not extend to cohabitation with a non–Jewess.[49] Consequently, the marriage in such cases does not constitute the lesser of two evils but, on the contrary, leads to transgressions of enhanced severity.

Furthermore, argues *Achi'ezer*, the prohibition against accepting insincere converts devolves upon the individual members of the *Bet Din.*[50] Hence, if the conversion is indeed undertaken for ulterior motives, the members of the *Bet*

Din are not permitted to commit a lesser infraction in order to spare another individual a graver transgression.[51]

Whatever the final adjudication of the Halakhah with regard to this complex question may be, in any particular case it can be seen that the permissibility of marriage under such circumstances constitutes a matter requiring careful Halakhic deliberation.

IV

The conversion problem has recently become a topical issue of major moment and has received a considerable measure of attention in both the general and Jewish press. As the prayerfully awaited Russian immigration turns from a trickle into a steady stream the question assumes new proportions since many of these new immigrants are accompanied by gentile spouses. These courageous new arrivals have endured untold hardships and manifested heroic self–sacrifice in effecting their exit from the Soviet Union. It is certainly fitting that every attempt be made to speed and ease their acculturation to life in Israel. When appropriate and Halakhically valid, the Israeli Chief Rabbinate has been most sympathetic in expediting the conversion process. Of late there has been an added attempt to ease procedural forms without prejudicing fundamental principles. In weighing the merits of such cases proper cognizance must be taken of all ramifications of the issue, of the practical problems it poses, and of the unique predicament of the Russian immigrants. However, in the last analysis, the question is purely one of Halakhic determination and certainly is not an area in which political pressure may be brought to bear.

Precisely such pressure raised the atmosphere in Israel to a fever pitch in the unfolding of events surrounding the celebrated Seidman case. At the time controversy raged with regard to the actions of Rabbi Shlomo Goren, Chief Chaplain of the Israeli armed forces. A feature article appearing in the weekend supplement of *Ha–Tzofeh*, 15 Sivan 5730, purports to give the rationale governing Rabbi Goren's actions in this case. It is reported that Rabbi Goren is of the belief that in Israel prospective proselytes are to be viewed differently from the way in which they are regarded in the Diaspora. "Beloved is the Land of Israel for it is receptive to converts," declares *Mesekhta Gerim* 4:3, in a tone remarkably different from that of the oft–quoted dictum of R. Chelbo, "Proselytes are as difficult for Israel as leprosy."[52] Noting that R. Chelbo's aphorism is not incorporated in the Palestinian Talmud, Rabbi Goren asserts that proselytization was frowned upon by the Sages in the Diaspora but welcomed in Israel. It is reported that Rabbi Goren, going a step further, asserts that in Israel sincerity of motivation may be dispensed with as a prior requirement for conversion. In the Diaspora converts motivated by reasons other than religious conviction cannot be accepted since doubts remain with regard to their future comportment; in Israel, where conversion entails not merely religious affiliation but national identification as well, such fears do not exist, contends Rabbi Goren. Hence, in his opinion, even converts prompted by self–serving motives may be accepted in Israel. This, Rabbi Goren argues, is the meaning of the declaration asserting that the Land of Israel is conducive to converts. Such converts, he maintains, automatically fall into the category of those of whom it may be confidently assumed that despite the absence of proper intent at the time of conversion nevertheless "their end will be for the sake of heaven."

Rabbi Goren's action in the Seidman case evoked disapprobation on the part of numerous rabbinic authorities who argued that his conclusions go far beyond what may be rigorously demonstrated on the basis of his sources. In fairness no detailed analysis of his argument can be undertaken until a published responsum penned by his own hand is available; journalistic accounts are most assuredly not a reliable basis for Halakhic evaluations.

One further point is worthy of note. One of the arguments militating against the conversion of Helen Seidman was the fact that Mrs. Seidman was a resident of an irreligious kibbutz in which dietary laws were flagrantly violated. Accordingly, there appeared to be reason to doubt the sincerity of her acceptance of *mitzvot*. The report in *Ha–Tzofeh* states explicitly that her candidacy was accepted by Rabbi Goren only on the basis of the fact that she was a vegetarian.[53] It would thus appear that there is nothing in Rabbi Goren's line of reasoning which condones acceptance of a proselyte who, we have reason to believe, does not intend to observe the precepts of Judaism.

In an article which appears in the current issue of *No'am* (5731), a similarly permissive stance is adopted by Rabbi I. Y. Unterman with regard to the spouses of Russian emigrés. Rabbi Unterman strongly emphasizes that throughout the period of his rabbinate in England he remained adamantly opposed to the acceptance of converts motivated by the desire for marriage to Jewish partners. While not altering his general position in this regard, Rabbi Unterman contends that the specific situation with regard to Russian immigrants to Israel is different on several counts. In the first place, the change in social and cultural climate in the wake of immigration to Israel engenders a commitment to Judaism which is absent in insincere converts in the Diaspora, Presumably Rabbi Unterman means that although conversions of this genre lack sincerity of motivation, such converts will ultimately accept the tenets of Judaism wholeheartedly and hence fall under the category of those whose conversion may be deemed to have been undertaken "for the sake of heaven." The counterargument which has been advanced against this position is that nationalistic identification should not be confused with religious commitment; willingness to share the destiny of Israel is not necessarily the same as an ultimate leap of faith in the God of Israel and commitment to His Torah. Secondly, argues Rabbi Unterman, rejection of such applicants may cause "a spiritual danger to hover over the entire family." The danger that the Jewish members of such families may be lost to Judaism, in Rabbi Unterman's opinion, creates a situation in which the regulations against accepting insincere converts may be suspended.[54]

While it is an axiomatic principle of Halakhah that each case in which a question arises must be decided in light of its own particular ramifications certain general principles emerge with striking clarity from the preceding discussion. It must be emphasized that a positive obligation exists with regard to candidates for conversion whose motivation is sincere. Such converts have always met with warm acceptance. However, conversions of convenience are not sanctioned by Halakhah and cannot be countenanced as a panacea designed to minimize the exacerbating problems posed by intermarriage. The situation with regard to converts who have no intention of observing the precepts of Judaism is even graver. The preponderance of halakhic opinion ranging from Reb Chaim Ozer to the late Chief Rabbi Herzog is that such conversions are null and void. It follows, of course, that the children of spurious female converts can also not be recognized as Jews in the eyes of Halakhah. The serious questions arising from such conversions should prompt a cautious attitude on the part of those whose duty it is to deal with these problems on a day–to–day basis, for it is they who are charged with safeguarding and preserving the identity of the Jewish people.

The halakhic strictures surrounding the acceptance of converts are but a reflection of the awesome burden and responsibility which accompanies membership in the community of Israel. One who lightheartedly seeks to join this community has no place in its ranks. "Israel," says the Almighty, "in you shall I glorify Myself." Such election is to be borne seriously and wholeheartedly or not at all. Only he who comes for no motive other than "the sake of heaven" may be permitted to become part of the Jewish people, affirming his solidarity not only with their past history and present fate but also with the totality of their faith, their traditions and their practices.

NOTES

1. *Shemot Rabbah Tezaveh* 36.
2. *Tanchuma, Lekh Lekha,*
3. II Kings 17:25–41.
4. Esther 8:17.
5. According to the interpretation of one authority, *Hagahot Mordekhai, Yevamot*, sec. 110, R. Nechemiah's view is not rejected but interpreted as having been expressed with regard to cases in which personal benefit is the sole motivating factor. According to this analysis R. Nechemiah accepts the validity of conversions which are motivated by a combination of ulterior considerations and "the sake of heaven."
6. *Mishneh Torah, Hilkhot Issurei Bi'ah* 13:14–15,
7. R. Isaac Schmelkes, *Teshuvot Bet Yitzchak, Yoreh De'ah*, II, no. 100, notes that Rambam carefully chooses the term *"bodkin acharav"* which connotes a careful investigation of the case, rather than the less inclusive *"bodkin oto"* which would indicate merely "examination" or interrogation of the applicant. The implication is that the *Bet Din* must make a full investigation of the facts and not rely upon the declaration of the candidate.
8. *Vide* R. Chaim Ozer Grodzinski, *Teshuvot Achi'ezer*, III, no. 26, sec. 2–3.
9. This interpretation is accepted and cited definitively by R. Joseph Karo in his commentary on the *Tur, Bet Yosef, Yoreh De'ah*, 268 and by *Shakh, Yoreh De'ah* 268:23, This leniency is, however, disputed by R. Ya'akov Ettlinger, *Binyan Zion*, no. 149.
10. *Kol Mevaser*, II, no. 8.
11. *Tuv Ta'am va–Da'at* I, no. 130. R. Shlomo Kluger, in a wider reaching statement, advances the opinion that in the event that the couple have cohabited even once, passion has been reduced and hence the conversion should not be viewed as being on account of man."
12. *Pri ha–Sadeh*, II, no. 3, and *Seridei Esh*, Ill, no. 50.
13. *Teshuvot Achi'ezer* III, no. 26, *Achi'ezer* indicates that possible ulterior motives must be determined by the *Bet Din* on the basis of individual circumstances. Fear of social ostracism or desire to share a common burial plot are also factors which, of course, must be weighed. *Vide Seridei*

Esh, III, no. 50. Desire for immigration to Israel as a possible ulterior motive is discussed by R. Isaac ha–Levi Herzog. *Teshuvot Heikhal Yitzchak*, Even *ha–'Ezer*, no. 21, sec. 2.

14. *Imrei Yosher*, I, no. 176, R. Yitzchak Ya'akov Weiss, *Minchat Yitzchak*, III, no. 101, concurs with the opinion expressed by *Imrei Yosher*.

15. *Binyan Zion*, no. 149.

16, *Menachem Meshiv*, no. 42.

17. R. David Hoffmann, *Melamed le–Ho'il Even ha–'Ezer*, no. 8, employs an identical line of reasoning in support of an even more radical contention. It is his opinion that in cases where the conversion is to the advantage of individuals other than the convert himself, the candidate may be accepted despite expressed reservations with regard to observance of a particular commandment. The case considered by Rabbi Hoffmann concerned a gentile woman who had been living with a Jewish husband for a considerable period of time. Conversion would have obviated the prohibition of consorting with a non–Jewess and would have legitimized the progeny of the Jewish husband. Rabbi Hoffmann, however, offers no supporting evidence for this innovative view.

18, *Chelkat Ya'akav*, I, no. 13.

19. *Cf.*, *Achi'ezer*, III, no. 26, sec. 7 and below note 48.

20. *Yoreh De'ah*, II, no. 100.

21. *Berakhot* 30.

22, *Achi'ezer*, III, no, 26, Sec. 2–3 and II, no. 28.

23. *Mishneh Torah, Hilkhat Issurei Bi'ah* 13: 17.

24. The concluding phrase of *Issurei Bi'ah* 13: 15 "*ad sheyeiraeh acharitam,*" lit. "until their end is known" is to be understood in the same vein. Accordingly, when quoted earlier it has been rendered, "until such time as their subsequent conduct could be observed."

A similar analysis of Rambam's exposition is advanced by R. Menachem Panet, *Avnei Zedek*, no. 27, Quoting Rambam and Ritva in their commentaries to *Kiddushin* 75b, *Avnei Zedek* declares that one who converts others than "for the sake of heaven" is deemed to be a convert after the fact only if it is known that he observes the precepts of Judaism even in private, Only when it becomes a ascertained that he is scrupulous in his observance is he considered with certainty to be a true proselyte; until such evidence is forthcoming his status is doubtful. The status of one who has no ulterior motive is never in doubt. Since there is no motivation for conversion other than sincere conviction he is immediately regarded as a true proselyte. *Avnei Zedek* employs this line of reasoning in offering a novel explanation of the underlying rationale governing the prohibition against marrying a convert with whom the prospective husband is suspected of having previously cohabited. The prohibition, asserts *Avnei Zedek*, is limited to a woman whose status is yet in doubt. A person of good character having knowledge of her private conduct may testify to her comportment as a pious Jewess and hence enter into marriage with the convert. One who has consorted with her, or who is suspected of having consorted with her while she was yet a gentile, is not deemed to be a reliable witness and hence may not marry her. He tentatively concludes that the prohibition is not operative if independent evidence of her personal piety is forthcoming. Cf., also R. Joseph Rosen, *Zofnat P'aneach, Issurei Bi'ah* 13:14, and R. Nathan Weidenfeld, *Teshuvot Chazon Nachum*, no. 90. A somewhat different analysis of Rambam's position is presented in *Heikhal Yitzchak, Even ha–'Ezer*, I, no, 20, sec. 2. Rabbi Herzog, however, agrees that marriage cannot be permitted even though the convert appears to observe the commandments of the Torah "until we come to a recognition of proper inner conviction."

A radically different interpretation is advanced by Rabbi Unterman in the current issue of *No'am* (5731) in the course of an essay entitled "*Hilkhot Gerut ve–Derekh Bitzu'an,*" pp. 1–9. Rabbi Unterman argues that conversions such as these are declared to be invalid by Rambam only if the convert subsequently reverts to the worship of foreign gods. In contradistinction to all authorities previously cited, Rabbi Unterman contends that subsequent failure to fulfill other halakhic obligations does not invalidate the conversion.

25. *Achi'ezer*, III, no. 26, sec. 4,

26. III, no. 28. This responsum also appeared in *Talpiot*, II (Sivan, 5705), no. 1–2.

27. *Achi'ezer* draws this distinction in order to resolve a fine point of halakhic reasoning. It may be contended that the candidacy of a woman who is known to have consorted with a Jew should be rejected out of hand if she intends to

marry him following conversion. In view of the fact that such marriage is forbidden by Rabbinic

edict, the prospective convert has, in effect, refused to accept one of the Rabbinic prohibitions, thereby disqualifying her candidacy
for conversion. *Achi'ezer* dismisses this argument by drawing a distinction between categorical rejection of an injunction and recognition that one will sin. *Melamed le-Ho'il, Even ha-'Ezer*, no. 8, raises the same question and resolves it on other grounds as indicated above. Since he recognizes the question as one which constitutes a serious conceptual problem and fails to advance the distinction formulated by *Achi'ezer* it may be deduced that Rabbi Hoffmann's position is in agreement with that of *Dvar Avraham* in opposition to the views of *Achi'ezer*. Cf., R. Yehudah Leib Kagan "*Hilkhot Gerim*," *Ha–Pardes*, XX (Sivan, 5706), no, 3, 30–33, and XX (Tammuz, 5706), no. 4, 29–31.
28. This letter was published by Rabbi Breish in the latter's *Chelkat Ya'akov*, I, no. 14. Similar sentiments are also expressed by Rabbi Herzog in his *Heikhal Yitzchak, Even ha–'Ezer*, I, no. 20, sec. 2 and no 21, sec. 3. Rabbi Herzog adds that if the candidate for conversion is a female the dangers are greater since an invalid conversion may cause grave ramifications with regard to subsequent marriage involving a Jewish partner and affect the genealogical purity of future generations.
29. *Chelkat Ya'akov* I, no. 13.
30. *Igrot Mosheh Yoreh De'ah*, no, 157.
31. *Igrot Mosheh, Yoreh De'ah*, no. 160.
32. *Yevamot* 24b.
33. Cf:, R. Joseph Colon, *Teshuvot Maharik*, no, 129 and R. Yosef Sha'ul Nathanson, *Sho'el u–Meshiv, Mahadurah Tinyanah*, III, no. 39 and *Binyan Zion*, no. 149.
34. Cf., R. Chaim of Zanz, *Teshuvat Divrei Chaim*, II, *Even ha–'Ezer*, no. 36, and *Achi'ezer*, III, no. 26. Both tentatively make this distinction but later state that cases of non–cohabitation are encompassed by Rashi's explanation. Their argument is that even according to Rashi subsequent marriage serves to intensify the scandal. *Achi'ezer* demonstrates this on the basis of the Tosefta which declares this prohibition to be binding with regard to an emancipated handmaiden even in cases where previous cohabitation is known with certainty to have occurred. Since, according to Rashi, no other rationale is applicable in the case of an emancipated female servant of whom no act of conversion is required (see below note 37). Rashi's intention must have been that when previous immorality is public knowledge subsequent marriage will enhance the scandal. R. Chaim Ozer suggests that in cases where the couple have undergone a civil ceremony there can be no further intensification of the scandal but subsequently rejects this line of reasoning since the Tosefta indicates that the prohibition remains effective even if the couple have sired children.
    Another interpretation of Rashi's opinion according to which Rashi forbids conversion in cases of definite cohabitation is offered by *Sho'el U'Meshiv, Mahadurah Tinyanah*, III, no, 39, According to this analysis, Rashi accepts the reasoning advanced by Rashba, i.e. that subsequent marriage would give rise to a well–founded suspicion that the conversion was motivated by a desire to facilitate such marriage, but regards this rationale as being limited solely to cases in which prior cohabitation is known to have occurred. Since such conversions are prohibited only before the fact but are efficacious when actually performed, Rashi, according to this interpretation, feels that there are no grounds on which to forbid subsequent marriages so long as there is no proof of prior cohabitation. Hence in the case to which specific reference is made in the Mishnah, i.e. one who is merely suspected of having previously cohabited with the woman in question, Rashi advances another reason, i.e. intensification of the scandal. Only after rumor becomes publicly accepted as a known fact does the fear that the woman will be suspected of having converted solely for the sake of marriage become an operative consideration.
35. No. 1205 of his collected responsa. Rashba's explanation is a bit problematic. Although it is forbidden to accept insincere candidates, nevertheless, such conversions are deemed valid when they become a *fait accompli*. If so, why is it necessary to protect the woman from the charge of insincerity since in any event her status as a Jewess will not be effected thereby? In resolving this problem *Achi'ezer* cites the words of Rashba in demonstrating that validity of conversion is contingent upon an acquiescent mental state. Conversions motivated by extraneous considerations are valid after the fact only if accompanied by an act of mental finality. If mental reservations exist the conversion is null and void. The ruling of the Mishnah regarding marriage is designed to eliminate the suspicion that such a mental state did not in fact exist which in turn would cast

doubt upon the status of the convert as a true Jewess.

36. In his previously cited responsum, sec. 4, R. Chaim Ozer speculates that conversion with the intention to marry under forbidden circumstances may in itself invalidate such conversion since such intention constitutes non–acceptance of a Rabbinic prohibition. Such reservation in and of itself is sufficient to nullfy any conversion. (Cf., however, *Heikhal Yitzchak, Even ha–'Ezer*, I, no. 19, sec. 2, who questions whether non–acceptance of a Rabbinic ordinance affects the Biblical validity of the conversion. The matter is left unresolved by Rabbi Herzog who fails to note that *Achi'ezer* unequivocally asserts that such

reservation nullifies the conversion. *Achi'ezer* maintains that such reservation is tantamount to non–acceptance of the Biblical injunction to heed the pronouncements of the Sages.) *Achi'ezer* notes, however, that the language of the Mishnah indicates that the prohibition regarding such a union devolves upon the husband rather than the wife. Hence the wife's violation is in the nature of "thou shalt not place a stumbling block before a blind person:" Accordingly, R. Chaim Ozer concludes that "perhaps" since the husband is not obligated to divorce her once the marriage is a *fait accompli*, the prohibition before the fact does not constitute a "stumbling block" and thus the woman has not declined to accept any obligation incumbent upon her.

R. Shlomo *Kluger, Tuv Ta'am va–Da'at*, I, no. 130, asserts that marriage is forbidden even if previous cohabitation is a certainty arguing that the prohibition would be farcical if it were applicable only to one who had not sinned, but was inapplicable in the case of an actual trans-gression–the transgressor cannot be permitted to gain by virtue of his trangression.

37. Both authorities note that Rashba is not concerned with providing an explanation for the prohibition with regard to emancipated handmaiden because he adopts the position of *Tosafot, Yevamot* 48a, to the effect that a slave cannot be forced to accept Judaism upon becoming the chattel of a Jew; hence if the slave has not previously done so he must accept the commandment of Judaism upon emancipation. Thus all considerations regarding voluntary acceptance of reli-gious obligations arc identical to those of ordinary converts. Rashi, on the other hand, is faced with a difficulty because of his disagreement with *Tosafot* in maintaining that obligation to fulfill precepts on the part of a slave is not contingent upon voluntary acceptance of the obligations of Judaism and hence no final acceptance of the "yoke of commandments" is ever required at the time of emancipation. Questions of sincerity are thus completely obviated.

For a different resolution of this difficulty with regard to Rashba's position see *Teshuvot R, Akiva Eger*, no, 121. Cf., also R. Yehudah Leib Graubart, *Chavalim Bane'imim*, III, no. 72 and R. Mordecai Winkler, *Levushei Mordekhai, Even ha.'Ezer*, no. 42.

38. *Igrot Mosheh, Even ha–'Ezer*, no. 27.

39, *Sho'el u–Meshiv, Mahadurah Tinyanah*, III, no. 39; *Binyan Zion*, no. 149; *Imrei Yosher*, I, no. 176.

40. *U'ke–Torah Ya'asu.*

41. *Even Yekara, Even ha–'Ezer*, no. 11.

42. *Melamed le–Ho'il, Even ha–'Ezer*, no. 10.

43. *Seridei Esh*, III, no. 50.

44. *Melamed le–Ho'il, Yoreh De'ah*, no. 85.

45. *Teshuvot Divrei Chaim*, II, *Even ha–'Ezer*, no. 36.

46, *Avnei Zedek*, no. 27, *Heikhal Yitzchak, Even ha–'Ezer*, I, no, 20, sanctions the conversion of a gentile woman who has already entered into a permanent relationship with a Jewish male on similar grounds, but only when it is known that the convert will observe the commandments of the Torah. A similar position is adopted by *Chavalim Bane'imim*, III, no. 72,

47. *Achi'ezer*, III, no. 72.

48. *P'er ha–Dor*, no. 132.

49. The Biblical prohibition of *niddah* applies only to a Jewess. However, the Hasmonean *Bet Din* issued a Rabbinic decree extending the *niddah* prohibition to a non–Jewess as well; *vide 'Avodah Zarah*, 36b. According to Rambam, *Mishneh Torah, Issurei Bi'ah* 12:2, this decree applies only in cases of a permanent relationship comparable to a common law marriage. The Biblical prohibition of *niddah* encompasses relations between a Jewess and a gentile male according to all authorities with the (possible) exception of Rabbenu Tam, *Sanhedrin* 74b, Cf., *Heikhal Yitzchak, Even ha–'Ezer*, I, no. 20, sec. 2. 50. *Chelkat Ya'akov*, I, no. 13, assumes an identical position with

regard to both points. Rabbi Breish adds that encouragement of conversion and subsequent marriage constitutes a disservice to the gentile consort. So long as the prospective convert remains a non–Jewess she commits no transgression in living with her Jewish consort–the transgression of cohabiting with a non–Jewess applies solely to the Jewish partner. However, after conversion, the *niddah* prohibition applies to both equally.

51. It is evident that R. David Hoffmann, *Melamed le-Ho'il, Even ha-'Ezer*, no. 8, adopted a contrary position and permitted this infraction on the part of the *Bet Din* in order to prevent illicit relations with a gentile. Cf., *Chelkat Ya'akov*, I, no. 13, who, while not quoting *Binyan Zion*, advances arguments contradicting this view. Rabbi Ettlinger, it should be noted, issued his permissive ruling only on condition that the couple scrupulously observe the laws of *niddah*; otherwise the prohibition attendant upon such a union are more severe following conversion. The case brought to his attention concerned a *kohen* who had already married a gentile in a civil ceremony and had fathered a son by his non–Jewish wife, *Binyan Zion* counselled conversion to be followed by the statutory ninety–day waiting period to determine prior pregnancy. However, since a *kohen* is not permitted to marry a proselyte, he advises that in order to mitigate the severity of their infraction they content themselves with a civil ceremony rather than nuptial rites in accordance with Jewish practice. According to many authorities, a Biblical violation of the priestly code occurs only if the marriage is solemnized in accordance with Jewish law.

52. *Yevamot 47b*.

53. However, this defense contains a specious element. Although he does not make specific reference to the Seidman case, Rabbi Unterman, *No'am*, p. 5. notes that even a vegetarian resident of an irreligious kibbutz must perforce violate the dietary laws by utilizing non–kosher utensils.

A second question with regard to Helen Seidman's acceptance of the "yoke of the commandments" is posed by the fact that her husband is a *kohen*. Marriage between a *kohen* and a convert is forbidden by Jewish law, This article alleges that Rabbi Goren sanctioned the marriage on the basis of "positions among the latter–day authorities" permitting such unions, Since it is universally recognized that Jewish law bans such marriages it would be most enlightening to know who the authorities are to whom reference is made. The Halaklah is clear: marriage between a kohen and a proselyte is forbidden.

54. This line of reasoning appears to be similar to the previously cited view of R. Shlomo Kluger who permitted conversion for the sake of marriage in the face of threatened apostasy on the part of the Jewish partner.

MY CHOSEN PEOPLE
Abraham Isaac Carmel

(EDITORIAL NOTE: Abraham Isaac Carmel was an extraordinary person who touched many thousands of people with the story of his spiritual search. He converted to Judaism in Great Britain, where he had been serving as a Roman Catholic priest, and soon thereafter went on *aliyah*. After a short time in Israel, he was forced to leave due to illness and came to the United States, where he taught English literature at the Yeshivah of Flatbush Joel Braverman High School. He died of cancer in 1982, a year after his retirement as a teacher, and was buried in Israel.

Mr. Carmel was an intense but private person whose sincerity and strength of commitment could not but impress all with whom he came into contact. He had traveled widely throughout the country, bringing his story to hundreds of communities and campuses. Whenever he spoke, he stressed the importance of strengthening Jewish education.

Mr. Carmel's spiritual autobiography is found in his book *So Strange My Path*. The following excerpts are from *My Chosen People*. a book he was working on at the time of his death. In it, he shares some of the frustration he felt as a convert, thoughts that he had not shared publicly before. The editors are grateful to the Yeshivah of Flatbush for making them available to the readers of TRADITION-JBW).

In July, 1943 I had been ordained Father Kenneth Charles Cox, in St. Mary's Cathedral, Edinburgh Scotland, by the Most Reverend Joseph MacDonald, of the Order of St. Benedict, Archbishop of St. Andrews and Edinburgh, Now, on the Eve of Yom Kippur, 1953, I was lying on an operating table in order to join myself through circumcision to the faith and people of Israel.

Thus I became the first fully-ordained priest in almost a thousand years to be received into Orthodox Judaism, I doubt whether any human being since the dawn of recorded history had felt more isolated, vulnerable, or utterly dependent upon the compassion of Almighty God. I was no less alone than the first men on the moon, One or two faithful friends communicated, as best they could, the goodness that was in their hearts, but they could not accompany me through the journey from earth's atmosphere, through spiritual space.

I had dared to cut history short in my own lifetime, and within a lifetime to encompass the whole of Jewish history. A proselyte, if he tries to live up to his calling, will re-live within his brief span the discrimination, hostility and callous cynicism experienced down the ages by those whom he has chosen as his people. Most cruel of all, he will find much of his suffering within that very family from which he had hoped to draw strength and consolation.

Students of Jewish history know very well that Jews are often embarrassed in the company of those who have presumed to claim as a privilege the "burdens" from which they themselves would gladly flee. If a Gentile marries a Jew, toleration can be granted in the case of those who go through a ceremony of conversion, but why should anyone be so stupid or presumptuous as to seek out Judaism in preference to another faith? This all too common attitude stems from an inferiority complex which many "born" Jews have inherited from centuries of persecution.

It would be sad enough if this complex were limited to the rank and file among the Jewish people, but it is strongest in the Jewish lay leadership, or should I say, the great mis-leadership that is only just beginning to disappear.

The most unfortunate example of discrimination on the part of the Jewish establishment has been the persistent refusal of the United Jewish Appeal to use me on behalf of Israel. On one occasion, when a community on Long Island insisted upon using me, I increased the sum from $32,000 to $65,000 over the previous year. So discrimination is not even profitable!

There is an incredible degree of arrogance in the Jewish autocracy and the time has come to challenge it. Many small men occupy very big jobs.

Most of my allies and truly genuine friends have been rabbis, They seemed to know from the clear message of Jewish tradition how greatly the proselyte needs encouragement if he is to survive, let alone succeed. The very few exceptions among rabbis have been those who were executives, rather than religious leaders or teachers.

I am particularly grateful for the opportunity of teaching, albeit humanities, to beautiful and gifted children, Perhaps the lay-leaders unintentionally did me a favor by excluding me from communal affairs!

Teaching is a rewarding task, but in America a teacher is a long way down the community ladder. He has no prestige or vital influence. American Jews in particular find it difficult to respect a person who is without financial backing. You are not quite kosher. If I were planning my life again, I would give more attention to material things and, above all, security. Idealism should be linked to a sense of financial adequacy.

I regret not having settled in Israel in 1960. When I take stock of my life since then, I doubt whether I have really gained anything by not remaining there. It is the proper place for an idealist, and the best of all places for a convert. Had I held on for a few more months, I might have recovered from my illness and continued my happy life. Even today I am constantly preoccupied with thoughts of her welfare and security.

My discovery of Judaism and my almost superhuman efforts to become one with the Jewish people constitute the only really worthwhile achievement of my life. It is the only area in which I feel no regrets, and if I had a thousand lives to live, I would want to succeed in this one goal at the expense, if necessary, of all others.

A SEPHARDIC BAN ON CONVERTS
S. Zevulun Lieberman

The Syrian–Sephardic Jewish community is one of the strongest homogeneous non–Hasidic Orthodox Jewish communities in the United States. The core of the community are descendants of early twentieth–century immigrants from Allepo, Syria, who (like their Ashkenazic brethren) came to New York's Lower East Side; along with the Allepean community came their sister community from Damascus. After a thirty–year period in Bensonhurst, the bulk of the community eventually settled in the Flatbush section of Brooklyn.

Over the decades, the community was joined by later immigrants from Syria, and more recently from Egypt and Lebanon. There is small community living in the area of Deal, New Jersey, where the majority of the Brooklyn community spends its summer vacation. Blessed with some fifty thousand souls, the community maintains a whole range of institutions, including synagogues, Yeshivot, a *beit din, kollelim, mikvaot* in Brooklyn and Deal, a *bikkur holim* society, a community center, a network of social institutions, and its own independent rabbinical council.

On an individual level, there is a wide range of religious observance; yet the sense of community is usually able to transcend these differences. It is rare to find a non–kosher home, and virtually all children receive a basic Jewish education, either at one of the community–sponsored yeshivot or at the Yeshivah of Flatbush (one third of whose students are Sephardic). Ideologically, the community is committed to Orthodoxy; a commitment to Torah and *hesed* permeates the every–day life of its institutions and members.

A close–knit pattern of social and economic inter–relationships motivates most people to marry within the community; indeed, better than ninety percent of the families are intra–communally married. However, it is the realization that no converts whatsoever will be accepted that keeps all but the most marginally affiliated from embarking upon serious social relationships with non–Jews. In 1935, following the example of the Syrian–Sephardic Jewish community of Argentina, the Brooklyn *beit din* promulgated a ban on accepting any converts; this was reaffirmed by the rabbinical authorities in 1946 and 1972.

These various proclamations were initiated by the community's rabbinical leaders. However, in 1984, sensing the increasing social pressures, the lay leaders initiated a public affirmation of the ban; they recognized it to be a necessary and effective tool for maintaining the social cohesiveness of the community.

The ban is based on the right of the community to promulgate *takkanot* and prohibitions. This is codified in the *Shulhan Arukh* and goes back to talmudic times, when Rav found a problematic situation regarding oaths in the Babylonian community: *Bik'a matsa ve–gadar gader*–"He found an open valley and built a fence."

The current situation in America regarding conversions, whereby most

37

gerut is done for the purpose of marriage, represents a sham and travesty of the Jewish tradition. But the Sephardic community's approach is proof of the power of a *kehilla* to protect its heritage and traditions, even though it may not be reproduceable across all American Jewish communities.

Our ban does not necessarily deny the legitimacy of any specific conversion; it does deny the convert and his or her Sephardic spouse (and their children) membership in the community. Of course, it does not apply to descendants of people who underwent a legitimate conversion prior to 1935 or to adopted children converted at birth.

What follows is an English translation of the Hebrew proclamations of 1935 and 1946, as well as the text of the 1984 proclamation.

A RABBINICAL PROCLAMATION
Adar 5695 (February 1935)

We have observed the conditions prevailing in the general Jewish community, where some youth have left the haven of their faith and have assimilated with non–Jews; in certain cases they have made efforts to marry gentiles, sometimes without any effort to convert them, and other times an effort is made for conversion to our faith, an action which is absolutely invalid and worthless in the eyes of the law of our Torah. We have therefore bestirred ourselves to build and establish an iron wall to protect our identity and religious integrity and to bolster the strong foundations of our faith and religious purity which we have maintained for many centuries going back to our country of origin, Syria.

We, the undersigned rabbis, constituting the Religious Court, together with the Executive Committee of the Magen David Congregation and the outstanding laymen of the community, do hereby decree, with the authority of our Holy Torah, that no male or female member of our community has the right to intermarry with non–Jews; this law covers conversions, which we consider to be fictitious and valueless. We further decree that no future rabbinic court of the community should have the right or authority to convert male or female non–Jews who seek to marry into our community. We have followed the example of the community in Argentina, which maintains a rabbinic ban on any of the marital arrangements enumerated above, an edict which has received the wholehearted and unqualified endorsement of the Chief Rabbinate in Israel. This responsa is discussed in detail in *Devar Sha 'ul, Yoreh Deah*, Part II to Part VI. In the event that any member of our community should ignore our ruling and marry, their issue will have to suffer the consequences. Announcements to this effect will be made advising the community not to allow any marriage with children of such converts. We are confident that the Jewish People are a holy people and they will adhere to the decision of their rabbis and will not conceive of doing otherwise.

Chief Rabbi Haim Tawil
Rabbi Jacob Kassin
Rabbi Murad Masalton
Rabbi Moshe Gindi
Rabbi Moshe Dweck Kassab

A SUBSEQUENT CLARIFICATION OF
THE ORIGINAL PROCLAMATION
Adar 5706 (February 1946)

On the 9th day of Adar I in the year 5706 corresponding to the 10th day of February, 1946, the rabbis of the community and the Committee of Magen David Congregation once again discussed the question of intermarriage and conversions. The following religious rabbinic decisions were promulgated and accepted:
1. Our community will never accept any converts, male or female, for marriage.
2. The rabbi will not perform any religious ceremonies for such couples, i.e., marriages, circumcisions, bar mitzvahs, etc. In fact, the Congregation's premises will be barred to them for use of any religious or social nature.
3. The Mesadrim of the Congregation will not accord any honors to the convert or one married to a convert, such as offering him an Aliyah to the Sefer Torah. In addition, the aforesaid person, male or female, will not be allowed to purchase a seat, permanently or for the holidays, in our Congregations.
4. After death of said person, he or she is not to be buried on the cemetery of our community, known as Rodfe Zedek, regardless of financial considerations.
   Seal of the Beth Din of Magen David Congregation.

Chief Rabbi Jacob S. Kassin

REAFFIRMING OUR TRADITION

WHEREAS, throughout the history of our community, our rabbis and lay leaders have always recognized the threat of conversions and the danger of intermarriage and assimilation; and have issued warnings and proclamations concerning these evils in February 1935, in February 1946 and in May 1972.

NOW, THEREFORE, we assembled rabbis and Presidents of the congregations and organizations of the Syrian and Near Eastern Jewish communities of Greater New York and New Jersey do now and hereby reaffirm these proclamations, and pledge ourselves to uphold, enforce and promulgate these regulations. We further declare that Shabbat Shuvah of each year be designated as a day to urge our people to rededicate themselves to these principles.

IN WITNESS WHEREOF, we have caused this document to be prepared and have affixed our signatures thereto, at a special convocation held on this third day of Sivan 5744 corresponding to the 3rd day of June, 1984.

Dr. Jacob S. Kassin
Chief Rabbi

The proclamation was signed by the rabbis and presidents of every synagogue, yeshivah, and social organization of the Sephardic Jewish communities of New York and New Jersey.

ANOTHER HALAKHIC APPROACH TO CONVERSIONS
Marc D. Angel

INTRODUCTION

In considering issues relating to the conversion of non–Jews to Judaism, Orthodox Jews tend to defend a strict policy which we term the Halakhic approach. Conversion for the sole purpose of marriage is highly discouraged. Conversion when the non–Jew does not intend to observe Halakhah in full is generally considered to be no conversion at all. Rabbi Melech Schachter, in a fine article on conversion, states what most Orthodox Jews believe:

> Needless to say, conversion to Judaism without commitment to observance has no validity whatever, and the spuriously converted person remains in the eyes of Halakhah a non–Jew as before.[1]

The purpose of this article is to present another Orthodox viewpoint on conversion. The traditional stringency is not the only Halakhically valid approach available to us; on the contrary, this may be the proper time to rely on other Halakhic standards. No one will argue that conversion to Judaism for other than spiritual reasons is ideal. Certainly it should be discouraged. However, in terms of practical reality we may have to be more tolerant of such conversions.

I

Raphael Hayyim Saban, then the Chief Rabbi of Istanbul, wrote to Rabbi Benzion Meir Hai Uziel, the Rishon Lezion, in 1943, asking if conversion for the sake of marriage is valid.[2] In his response, Rabbi Uziel opens with a quotation from the *Shulkhan Arukh (Yoreh Deah*, 268: 12) which states that we must examine a potential convert to determine if his motives for accepting Judaism are sincere. Certainly, the ideal is not to convert those who are insincere. Then Rabbi Uziel adds that since in our generation intermarriage is common in civil courts, we are often forced to convert the non–Jewish partner in order to free the couple from the prohibition of intermarriage. We must also do so in order to spare their children who would otherwise be lost to the Jewish fold.[3] If we are faced with a *de facto* mixed marriage we are permitted to convert the non–Jewish spouse and the children, when applicable. If this is true when the couple is already married, it is obviously true before they have begun a forbidden marriage relationship. The conversion could offset future transgressions and religious difficulties.

41

Rabbi Uziel bases his opinion on a responsum of the Rambam.[4] The case before Maimonides dealt with a Jewish man who had a non–Jewish maid–servant. The man was suspected of having conducted himself immorally with his servant. Should the *bet din* have her removed from his house? In his answer, the Rambam states categorically that according to the law the maid should be sent out. After it learned of his wrongs, *bet din* was obligated to exert all its power either to have the maid sent out or to have the Jewish master free her and then marry her. But there is a law stating that if one is suspected of having had immoral relations with his maid and then he freed her he may not marry her.[5] The Rambam said that in spite of the ruling, he has judged in such cases that the man should free her and marry the maid. He justified his decision by stating that it is necessary to make things easier for repentants (*Takanat Hashavim*). He relied on the famous statement of our rabbis, "It is time to serve the Lord, go against your Torah." The Rambam closed this responsum with a significant, profoundly religious comment, "and the Lord in His mercy will forgive our sins . . ."[6]

The Rambam recognized that his decision is in violation of the ideal Halakhic standard. However, he allowed his human insight to cope with the problem realistically, and he invoked other Halakhic standards to justify himself. As a true man of reason and faith, he dealt with the situation sensibly while relying on God's mercy. God will understand the motivations for this Halakhic decision and will either approve or forgive. In any case, what must be done will be done.

In support of the Rambam's approach, Rabbi Uziel cites several Talmudic sources which reflect the same attitude.[7] It is better to choose the lesser of two evils, even when the choice is not ideal. It is better to stop adding fuel to evil now, rather than to risk an increase of transgression.

Based on this attitude, Rabbi Uziel says that when an intermarried couple comes to a *bet din* seeking the conversion of the non–Jewish partner, we must allow such a conversion. We may not take the haughty position that these are wicked people who deserve to suffer the fate of transgressors.[8] On the contrary, by coming to Halakhic authorities the couple display a desire to avoid transgression. They do not want to reject the Torah but want to be included in the Jewish community.

As was stated earlier, if we are permitted to convert one who is already married to a Jewish mate, we may certainly convert one who wishes to marry a Jewish partner in the future. Even if we know that the main and perhaps only reason for the conversion is marriage, yet when all is said and done such a conversion is still Halakhically valid.[9]

But Rabbi Uziel considers such conversions not only to be permissible, but actually morally required. Rabbis are not only allowed to convert a non–Jew for purposes of marriage, but are urged not to step away from the positive responsibility to do so. In support of this idea, Rabbi Uziel referred to the strict chastisements of the prophet Malachi against those who married out of the faith.

> Judah has dealt treacherously, and an abomination is committed in Israel and in Jerusalem; for Judah has profaned the holiness of the Lord which He loves and has married the daughter of a strange god. May the Lord cut off to the man that does this . . . (Malachi, 2:11–12).

In view of the stringent prohibition of marrying a *bat el nehar* Rabbi Uziel argues that it is better to convert the non–Jewish partner so that the Jewish partner could be spared from this severe transgression. Such conversion is also better for the children who would be born to the couple since they could now be considered legally as Jews. Considering the alternatives of conversion or intermarriage, Rabbi Uziel ruled in favor of conversion.

Rabbi Uziel, however, qualifies his opinion in that he feels that the judges should do everything they can to break off the projected marriage and resort to conversion only when it is clear that the couple definitely will not be disuaded. The judges should direct their heart to God when they perform the conversion, and "the merciful God will forgive."

In 1951, Rabbi Uziel received a question from Yehudah Leon Calfon, a rabbi in Tetuan. The problem involved was: may we convert the non–Jewish wife and children of a Jewish man when he is not observant and does not sincerely intend to have his family be observant? If a Jew observes the *mitzvot* like the average Jew of his time (*Kistam Yehudim bazeman hazeh*) then there would be no problem since we could rely upon the responsum of the Rambam. But what about the Jew who does not observe *Shabbat, Yom–Tov, Kashrut*, etc. Shall we prohibit the conversions or shall we say that since the Jew still wants to be included in the Torah community–albeit to a limited extent–we may convert his non–Jewish wife and children?[10]

Following a preliminary discussion, Rabbi Uziel comes to grips with this serious problem. He refers to our standard procedure when a non–Jew comes to convert. We teach him the principles of Judaism–unity of God, prohibition of idol worship. We inform him of some of the easy and difficult *mitzvot*, as well as some of the rewards and punishments. We do not teach him everything. The Shakh comments that we do not tell the would–be convert all the technicalities and stringencies because we might scare him away. If he is really sincere about his wish to convert, it would be wrong to frighten him out of his desire.[11]

From this standard procedure, we see that there is no requirement to ask the non–Jew actually to observe the *mitzvot*. We do not require his assurances that he will be an observant Jew. If we did, we could never have any converts, because no *bet din* can guarantee absolutely that the convert will keep all the *mitzvot*. The reason we tell the non–Jew some of the *mitzvot* is to give him an idea of what is involved in becoming an observant Jew. That way, he may have the option to change his mind about conversion. If, however, he converts and does not observe, he is considered as a Jew who transgresses.

Moreover, the procedure of informing the non–Jew about basic beliefs and *mitzvot* is required initially. However, if we did not follow the procedure and we converted the non–Jew anyway (circumcision and ritual immersion), the conversion is valid notwithstanding.[12]

Rabbi Uziel remarks that if a non–Jew gives us no indication that he expects to observe the *mitzvot*, we may still convert him even initially.[13] It is not only permitted to accept converts on this basis, but it is also a *mitzvah* upon us to do so. We, of course, hope that they will observe and we should encourage them to keep the *mitzvot*. But if they do not, they are still Halakhically considered to be Jews.[14]

There is an argument that since the vast majority of converts today do not observe the *mitzvot* even for a short time, we should not accept converts at all. To the Rabbi Uziel replies that it is a *mitzvah* to accept converts.[15] Furthermore, it is dangerous to forbid conversion since it will force the Jewish partners of inter–faith marriages either to convert to the other religion or to become defiled by the improper relationship. Those who have been rejected from the people of Israel have historically been our worst enemies. We also have an obligation to the children of these marriages. After all, they are of Jewish stock (*Mizera Yisrael*) even if their mother is not Jewish. They are lost sheep whom we must reclaim for our people.

In an emotional passage, Rabbi Uziel writes:

> And I fear that if we push them (the children) away completely by not accepting their parents for conversion, we shall be brought to judgment and they shall say to us: 'You did not bring back those that were driven away, and those who were lost you did not seek"
>
> (Ezekiel, 34:4).

This chastisement is far more severe than the chastisement of accepting converts who in all likelihood will not be observant Jews.[16]

From these responsa it is clear that Rabbi Uziel offers a Halakhic perspective which reflects a profoundly sympathetic and understanding spirit. Recognizing the practical realities of our world, it is essential that Halakhic authorities courageously respond to the needs. Ours must not be a haughty and elite attitude towards would–be converts. We have a moral obligation to convert those who seek conversion, not only for their sakes but of the sakes of their children. Of course, we must make every effort to teach them the Torah and to encourage their adherence to the *mitzvot*. But in the final analysis, we must put our faith in human reason and compassion, and, certainly, we must put our faith in God (*Vehu Rachum Yekhaper . . .*).

NOTES

1. *Jewish Life*, May–June, 1965 p. 7. See also p. 11, under the heading, "Commitment to Total Observance."
2. *Mishpetei Uziel*, Jerusalem, 1964, No. 18.
3. See Rabbi Schachter, *op. cit.*, p. 13.
4:. *Pe–er Hador*, Amsterdam, 1765, No. 132. See also *Mishpetei Uziel*, *op. cit.*, No. 21, where Rabbi Uziel also relies on this Rambam.
5. See T.B. *Yebamot*, 24b.
6. הנטבל על השפחה ונשתחררה אינו יכול לישאנה *לכתחילה.*
ופסקנו כך מפני תקנת השבים ואמרנו מוטב שיאכל רוטב ולא שומן עצמו
וסמכנו על אומרם ז"ל עת לעשות לד' הפרו תורתיך ויכול לישאנה והקל
ברחמין יכפר עונינו כאשר דבר לנו ואסירה כל בדילייד.

7. T .B. *Kiddushin*, 21 b. מוטב שיאכלו בני ישראל בשר תמותות שחוטות ואל יאכלו בשר נבילות תמותות.
T .B. *Shabbat*, 31b. דרש עולא מאי דכתיב אל תרשע הרבה, מי שאכל שום וריחו נודף יאכל עוד שום.
8. Rabbi Uziel says that the concept of הליעיטהו לרשע וימת (T.B. *Baba Kama*, 69a) does not apply here.
9. T.B. *Yebamot*, 24b. The question is: is a person who converts for דבר אחר a real convert? The conclusion is that he is הלכה כדברי האומר כולם גרים הם.

44

This is brought down in the codes. See for example, the *Mishneh Torah* of Maimonides, *Hilkot Isurei Biah*, 13:17: and the Tur, *Yoreh Deah*, 268.

10. *Mishpetei Uziel, op. cit.*, No. 20.

11. *Yoreh Deah*, 268, *Se–if katan*, 5.

12. See the Shakh, *Se–if katan*, 3.

13. מכל האמור למדנו: שאין תנא' קיום המצוות מעכב את הגרות אפילו לכתחילה.

See the *Shulkhan Arukh*, Y.D. 268, 2 and 12.

14. מכל האמור ומדובר תורה יוצאה שמותר ומצוה לקבל גרים וגיורות אע"פ שידוע לנו שלא יקיימו כל המצוות משום שסופם יבואו לידי קיומם ומצווים אנו לפתח להם פתח כזה ואם לא יקיימו את המצוות הם ישאו את עונם ואנו נקיים.

15. T.B. *Yebamot*, 109b, *Tosafot*, "Ra–ah."

16. For other of Rabbi Uziels responsa on conversion see, *Mishpetei U'tel, op. cit.*, No. 22: *Mishpetei Uziel*, Vol .1, *Yoreh Deah*, No. 14; *Mishpetei Uziel*. Vol. 2. *Eben Ha 'Ezer*. No. 25.

CONVERSION IN JEWISH LAW
Shlomo Riskin

INTRODUCTION

Attitudes towards conversion is one of the most crucial issues confronting Judaism today. The Jewish community in America has been irrevocably bifurcated since Orthodox rabbis will not perform a marriage between a "natural" Jew (one born to a Jewish mother or converted in accordance with Jewish law) and one "converted" by a Conservative or Reform rabbi not in strict accordance with Halakhah, Jewish law. The "Who is a Jew" controversy in Israel has bitterly divided the religious parties and has caused untold animosity between the religious and non–religious camps. The secularists agonizingly cry: Is the Russian emigre married to a Christian, who has risked life and limb to leave the "Communist paradise" and re–establish historic ties in Israel, to be told that his children are not Jews and cannot be married in a religious ceremony? Is the Israeli kibbutznik who was born to Christian parents but who has placed her destiny with Israel's future and who has worked and fought for Israel's development to be denied the status of a Jew merely because she did not undergo some *pro forma* rite of acceptance? And the religionist staunchly responds: We must maintain the sanctity of Israel! Our faith commitment is based upon a precise legal system which has been responsible for the preservation of our people these three thousand years. We dare not compromise our halakhic standards.

And even within the Orthodox camp there is a good deal of ferment over the exact meaning of "conversion in accordance with Jewish law." The "lightning" conversion of Helen Seidman, *chaverah* of an irreligious kibbutz and married to a *Kohen*, which was arranged by Rav Shlomo Goren, the then Chief Chaplain of the Israeli Armed Forces and presently Ashkenazic Chief Rabbi of Israel, caused a storm of controversy throughout Israel and the Diaspora.[1] In an article in *TRADITION* (Spring 1971) by J. David Bleich entitled, "The Conversion Crisis: A Halakhic Analysis," the author asserts on the basis of numerous responsa that

> all authorities agree that an application for conversion may justifiably be entertained only if the *Bet Din* is satisfied that upon conversion the candidate will become a God–fearing Jew and will scrupulously observe the commandments of the Torah . . . Where it is evident that the candidate will be non–observant, the conversion is null and void despite the candidate's oral declaration of acceptance of the yoke of *mitzvot*.[2]

47

And in the recent Langer controversy, Rav Goren suggests in a published responsum that a convert who does not live in accord with Jewish law but reverts to his original practices thereby nullifies the act of conversion.[2a] But two issues later in *TRADITION* (Winter–Spring 1972) Marc D. Angel wrote "Another Halakhic Approach to Conversions," in which he asserts in the name of Rav Uziel, former Rishon Lezion, that

> there is no requirement to ask the non-Jew actually to observe the mitzvot. We do not require his assurance that he will be an observant Jew . . .[3]

And at a recent Mizrachi forum a popular Orthodox Rabbi, in an attempt to empathize with the plight of the Israeli secularists, queried:

> Should not conversion by fire be at least as acceptable to Jewish tradition as conversion by water? [4]

I shall attempt in this essay to clearly outline the halakhic requirements for conversion as they are expressed in the Talmud, Rishonim and the codes. Then we shall have the necessary basis to understand the various attitudes cited in the responsa and hopefully begin to chart the most sensible. approach to conversion for our own times.

I

Prima facie, the Talmudic sources would seem to indicate that circumcision for males and ritual immersion for males and females are the necessary prerequisites for conversion without even a mention of acceptance of commandments. It is written in the Talmud:

> Whether he had performed ritual ablution but had not been circumcised or whether he had been circumcised but had not performed the prescribed ritual ablution, he is not a proper proselyte, unless he has been circumcised and has also performed the prescribed ritual ablution.[5]

The Talmud continues along this vein:

> R. Oshaia b. Hiyya taught that there came before him a proselyte who had been circumcised but had not performed the ablution. He told him, "Wait here until tomorrow when we shall arrange for your ablution." From this incident three rulings may be deduced. It may be inferred that the initiation of a proselyte requires the presence of three men; and it may be inferred that a man is not a proper proselyte unless he had been circumcised and had also performed the prescribed ablution; and it may also be inferred that the ablution of a proselyte may not take place during the night.[6]

To be sure, the Talmud does describe a procedure of informing the would-be convert of the sacrifices entailed in becoming a Jew:

> Our Rabbis taught: If at the present time a man desires to become a proselyte, he is to be addressed as follows: "What reason have you for desiring

48

to become a proselyte; do you not know that Israel at the present time is persecuted and oppressed, despised, harassed and overcome by afflictions?" If he replies, "I know and yet am unworthy," he is accepted forthwith, and is given instruction in some of the minor and some of the major commandments; and several of the more stringent commandments. And as he is informed of the punishment for the transgression of the commandments, so is he informed of the reward granted for their fulfillment. He is not, however, to be persuaded or dissuaded too much. If he accepted, he is circumcised forthwith. As soon as he is healed arrangements are made for his immediate ablution, when two learned men must stand by his side and acquaint him with some of the minor commandments and with some of the major ones. When he comes up after his ablution he is deemed to be an Israelite in all respects.[7]

Apparently, therefore, it is the task of the Jewish court about to accept the proselyte to inform him of the difficulties of Jewish destiny as well as of the particulars of some of the commandments. Nevertheless, the great codifier Maimonides, while he clearly expressees the initial necessity of investigating the would be convert to ascertain his sincerity as well as of informing the would–be convert of the substance of the yoke of Torah,[8] concludes:

A proselyte, after whom the *Bet Din* did not investigate or to whom they did not inform the particulars of the commandments and their punishments, but who was circumcised and ritually immersed before three common judges, is considered a convert. And even if they discover that it was for some ulterior motive that he converted, since he was circumcised and ritually immersed he has left the category of Gentile . . . And even if he returns (to his former ways) and serves idols he is considered an apostate Jew whose marriage is a marriage.[9]

At least according to this authority, it would seem that conversion is–if only *post–facto*–a *pro–forma* ritual of circumcision and ritual immersion which takes effect even without the judges having informed the would–be proselyte of the particulars of his Jewish status. This is the basis of the responsum of Rav Uziel, and this might lead us to believe that acceptance of commandments is a desirable but not necessary constituent of conversion.

II

I must strongly disagree with the conclusion, and a more intensive study of the sources will demonstrate that the acceptance of commandments is a far more integral part of conversion than might appear. The Talmud, in a totally different context from the general discussion of conversion, quotes a *beraita*:

Our Rabbis taught . . . If a heathen is prepared to accept the Torah except one religious law, we must not receive him (as an Israelite).[10]

Following the discussion of circumcision and ritual ablution, the Talmud contrasts the laws of a proselyte and an emancipated slave. The acceptance of the yoke of commandments may apply only to a proselyte, argues the Talmud, apparently assuming the acceptance of commandments as a basic element of conversion.[10a] It is apparently on this basis that the *Baalei Tosafot* go so far as to state that although the ritual immersion of the convert may not require the presence of three judges, the acceptance of the commandments–even *post facto*–does require their presence.[11] This is especially significant since the context of the Talmud upon which *Tosafot* was commenting had not so much as mentioned the term "acceptance of commandments." And Rav Yosef Karo, the author of the authoritative *Yoreh Deah*, bases his decision upon this principle:

> All matters pertaining to the convert, whether it be informing him of the commandments for their acceptance, circumcision or ritual immersion, must be performed in the presence of three qualified judges and during the day. However, this is only necessary initially. *Post facto*, if he were circumcised or ritually immersed before two judges or at night–and even if the immersion were not for the sake of conversion (but, for example, had been because of ritual purity)–the individual is a convert and may marry an Israelite. (This is with the) exception of the acceptance of commandments which prevents conversion if it does not take place in the presence of three (qualified judges) and by day.[12]

Both the *Schach* and *Taz* explain this insistence of the *Yoreh Deah* on three qualified judges for the acceptance of the commandments on the principle that: "This is the essence of the matter (of conversion) and its first step."

III

I would submit that even according to Maimonides the acceptance of commandments is a necessary prerequisite for conversion. As mentioned previously, Maimonides insists that initially the would–be convert must be carefully investigated–and informed of the various obligations incumbent upon him as a Jew. And even if *post facto* the informing of the individual commandments does not disqualify the conversion, the lack of general acceptance of commandments certainly would. Indeed, Maimonides never mentions the acceptance of commandments as a necessary prerequisite for conversion. It is rather the very definition of conversion, the statement of purpose, the matrix from which circumcision and ritual immersion must follow.

> And so for generations when a gentile wishes to enter into the covenant, to be encompassed by the wings of the Divine Presence and *to accept upon himself the yoke of Torah*, he requires circumcision and ritual immersion . . .[13]

And so Maimonides affirms the aforementioned Talmudic statement that "even if an individual accepted upon himself the entire Torah with the, exception of one detail, he may not be accepted for conversion,"[14] since the acceptance of commandments in principle is the very essence of the conversion procedure.

Perhaps this may be analogous to commandments such as the recitation of the *Shema* or rejoicing during the Festival. In each case there are certain mechanical performances clearly prescribed by Jewish law: The recitation of certain paragraphs at specific times each day for the one, the eating of meat and drinking of wine for the other (*maasei mitzvah*). But without the commitment of the acceptance of the yoke of the heavenly kingdom accompanying the mouthing of the halakhically ordained words of the *Shema,* without the internal feelings of joy which are to be expressed by the eating and drinking unique to the Festival, the commandments cannot be considered fulfilled (*Kiyum Hamitzvah*). Similarly circumcision and ritual immersion without the concomitant acceptance of commandments become meaningless mechanical performances and are to no avail as far as conversion is concerned.[15] In sum therefore, Maimonides may *post facto* accept a conversion which lacked the informing of commandments (*hodaat hamitzvot*), but he would not accept a conversion which lacked the acceptance of commandments (*kabbalat hamitzvot*).[16]

IV

I cannot accept an essential distinction between the acceptance of commandments and the observance of commandments. It is self–understood that no Jewish court can guarantee future actions of the convert. Nevertheless it is to be expected that the expressed acceptance of commandments implies the willingness on the part of the convert to live in accordance with the scrupulous observance of these commandments for the rest of his life. Unlike Christianity; Judaism has never recognized a faith commitment apart from its tangible expression in deed. Whether or not there actually exists a commandment to believe in God is questioned by the various Biblical commentaries,[17] whereas the entire halakhic process bespeaks an emphasis upon proper observance as the necessary expression of sincere faith. The convert who accepts the commandments is expected to observe them.[18]

Were the acceptance and subsequenut observance of commandments not an inextricable aspect of conversion, the status of the proselyte who converted with ulterior motives would never have been questioned by the Talmud. Although we conclude that *post facto* all those who converted for ulterior motives are valid converts,[19] Hillel and R.. Chiya accepted such converts initially because, explains the *Baalei Tosafot,* "they knew that ultimately they would be complete proselytes."[20] There is therefore a degree of latitude accorded the individual court to decide as to the ultimate sincerity of the specific convert[21] sincerity as to his halakhic observance.

There is one more Halakhah which demonstrates the close relationship between conversion and acceptance and observance of commandments. The Talmud teaches that a minor may be converted by the consent of a Jewish court, in whose presence he is circumcised and ritually immersed:

> Rabbi Joseph says: When he comes of majority age, he may reject (the conversion). But once he has attained the age of majority for one hour and does not reject (the conversion), he may no longer reject it.[22]

Apparently the one element lacking in the conversion of the minor was the acceptance of the commandments, since this cannot be performed for a minor (as can ritual immersion and circumcision), but must be attested to by an adult. Hence Rabbi Joseph gives him the option of rejecting the conversion upon his achievement of majority status. Interestingly enough, the *Rosh* interprets Rabbi Joseph as follows:

> R. Joseph says: When he comes of majority age he may reject (the conversion) *before we saw him observing the religion of Judaism*. But on the day he achieves majority and we saw him fulfilling the commandments, he can no longer reject the conversion.[23]

The *Yoreh Deah* cites the halakhah in accordance with the interpretation of the *Rosh*.[24] Hence we clearly see the necessity of acceptance of commandments and an insightful equation of acceptance of commandments and observance of commandments. The observance *ipso facto* testifies as to the acceptance, and the conversion thereby becomes validated and can never again be denied.[25] Therefore whereas it may not be necessary to inform the would–be convert of every detailed aspect of the Jewish life–style, a general acceptance of commandments is a necessary prerequisite for conversion.

V

The modern issue of "Who is a Jew" is fraught with implications for the future of our people. The real issue at stake is not "Who is a Jew?" but "What is a Jew?" It is fashionable in this Age of Anxiety to undergo an identity crisis, and unfortunately Judaism is involved in that same crisis. For the majority of Americans, religion is at most a once–a–week sentiment but more generally a dose of morality for the children with a family dinner a few times a year to mark the major holidays. *"Vie se christelt sich, so yidelt sich,"* and so the pediatric Hebrew School, the nostalgic High Holy Days, the gastronomic seder and the U.J.A. bagels–and–lox breakfast have become the hallmark of American Jewry. If you add a little Zionism and a number of fund–raising dinners each year, you have the total picture of what Judaism means to the majority of affiliated Jews. With this backdrop it is no wonder that ten lectures devoted to Jewish History and Culture with a signed certificate and name–giving ceremony can make any WASP into a HASP (Hebrew Anglo–Saxon Protestant) within a few short months.

The existence of the State of Israel compounds the problem, since most Israelis are so intoxicated with being like the other nations, (perhaps understandably so after a 2,000 year–long diaspora and four difficult wars for existence), that they have forgotten our ideal to be "a light unto the other nations." Feelings of Israeli nationalism run high, and the deepest Jewish goal tends to be identified with the needs of the Israeli nation. *Klal Yisrael* and *Medinat Yisrael* have become a singular entity. It therefore seems imperative that any individual merging his destiny with the Jewish State be entitled to call himself Jew and to wear that appellation with pride, no matter what rituals he may or may not have undergone.

Jewish history viewed with religious perspective would deny both the sentimental and the nationalistic view of Jewish identity. We first became a nation at Sinai, and, as Rabbenu Saadia Gaon so aptly wrote: "We exist as a nation only by virtue of our Torah." We have managed to survive as a people for two thousand years, albeit with great difficulties, without a homeland, but we cannot survive for four generations without Torah adherence. Judaism does have a unique message for the world, but that message cannot be expressed in pious platitudes about the Judeo–Christian tradition of the Golden Rule. Judaism is based upon commitment, an often sacrificial and always profound commitment to a legal system which endows every step of life (halakhah) with direction (Torah) and transcendence. Our ethical and moral *weltanschauung* is expressed in terms of Sabbath, Festivals, *kashrut*, and ritual purity. We strive to create a kingdom of priests and a holy nation which will ultimately serve as a model for the entire world to follow. Since the stirring Biblical epic of the sacrifice of Isaac, the ideal of the Jew has been not to die for Judaism but rather to live by the direction of our faith. It is a commitment to this total way of life which has preserved Judaism through the ages, and it is the kind of commitment which must be asked of any individual who wishes to join our ranks. Circumcision and ritual immersion are the formal acts by which the would–be convert demonstrates his willingness to sacrifice himself in life and to become symbolically reborn into a new faith community; the acceptance of commandments is the very essence of his conversion.

VI

There are, however, two concerns which must be discussed. Many Orthodox rabbis are often unsympathetic and even harsh with the would–be convert who seeks guidance. Undoubtedly we have certain standards, and these standards must be maintained. Nevertheless, if one comes to be purified, we–in the spirit of *imitatio dei*–must be ready to offer assistance. There are authorities who subsume the acceptance of the proselyte under the Biblical command of "Thou shalt love the stranger,"[26] and one authority even insists that it is included in "Thou shalt love the Lord thy God with all thy heart"–cause Him to be beloved by all the creatures (of the world) as (did) Abraham our father. [27] And the Talmud goes so far as to state that Amalek, the arch enemy of Israel, was a descendant of Timna, who had been rejected for conversion by our patriarchs. Had she but been accepted at the proper time, the entire subsequent history of Israel would have been radically different . . . I would recommend that a special Institute for Proselytes be established, preferably under the auspices of the Rabbinical Council of America, to provide a proper course of study as well as practical guidance in the observance of commandments for the would–be convert. It has been my practical experience that many young people have become genuinely attracted to authentic Jewish life, and even those who may initially approach our door for the sake of marriage will quickly become righteous proselytes under the proper tutelage. In the cases where a potential marriage partner is the initial cause of interest, it is imperative that the Jew as well as the Gentile attend the Institute together. I would insist upon the Jew's commitment to accept the commandments along with the convert's. A proper court of three Rabbis would, of course, judge each instance to ascertain the sincerity of the applicant in accord with the decision of the codes.[29] In the absence of such an Institute for Proselytes we are causing countless individuals to turn to invalid forms of conversion for themselves and their loved ones which results in heartbreak and irretrievable loss to our people.

VII

The second issue of concern is the treatment of the proselyte by the Jewish community. The Talmud teaches that Torah is not a biological inheritance, and there are those who maintain that there are forty–six Biblical injunctions against anyone who behaves improperly towards a convert.[30] Indeed, the Book of Ruth, which is read on the Festival of Torah, *Shevuot*, conveys as its primary message the irrelevance of genealogy for true Jewish leadership. Ruth was born a Moabite woman, and Moab had originally been conceived as a result of the heinous act of incest between Lot and his daughter. Boaz descended from Perez, the result of a forbidden relationship between Yehudah and his daughter–in–law Tamar. But as long as halakhah permits Boaz and Ruth to wed, they become the progenitors of no less a personage than King David, psalmist of the Lord, architect of Jerusalem, progenitor of the Messiah.

The Book of Ruth attempts to instruct the Jewish people to accept the sincere proselyte with sensitivity and compassion. Even after her conversion, Ruth is regarded by the Bethlemites as a Moabite woman, [31] and so she is regarded at best with disdain and at worst with contempt. Ruth even regards herself as a stranger as a result of the Israelite treatment, and she therefore responds to Boaz's kindness with:

> Why have I found favor in thy sight, that thou shouldn't take cognizance of me, seeing I am a foreigner?[32]

Boaz expresses the proper attitude towards the convert in his response, strongly reminiscent of God's initial command to the very first proselyte, Abraham our Father:

> It have fully been told me . . . how thou has left thy father and thy mother, and the land of thy nativity, and art come unto a people that thou knowest not heretofore.[33] The Lord recompense thy work, and be thy reward complete from the Lord, the God of Israel, under whose wings thou art come to take refuge.[34]

The proof that Ruth is to be regarded as a genuine Jewess lies in the affirmation of the obligation of the next of kin to marry her and thereby *preserve* the seed of her deceased husband. It is as a reminder of his obligation that Naomi sends Ruth to visit Boaz at the threshing floor. The nearest kinsman agrees to redeem the sold fields of the family of Elimelech, but refuses to marry Ruth "lest I destroy mine own inheritance." He apparently still regards the convert as a stranger, and cohabitanting with her would produce not a preservation of seed but a destruction of seed, an eternal impurity in the biology of his family. Boaz understands the validity of the true conversion, views Judaism as transcending biology alone, weds Ruth and is worthy of becoming the grandfather of the Messiah. Indeed, it is the vision of the Messianic Age that the entire world will unite to learn Torah, convert to the Jewish doctrine and live in peace and amity. [35]

And as Boaz teaches with what compassion we must accept the convert. Ruth teaches the formula for acceptance of commandments. Her statement of faith to the religious Naomi includes commitment to action as well as to ideals, allegiance to God as well as to nation, commitment to live as a Jew as well as to die as one:

> for whither thou goest, I will go and where thou lodgest, I will lodge; thy nation shall be my nation and thy God my God; where thou diest will I die, and there will I be buried . . .[36]

NOTES

1. Unfortunately. Rav Goren has not yet penned a responsum explaining his action. A feature article which appeared in the week–end supplement of *Hatzofeh*, 15 Sivan 5730, purports to present his major halakhic considerations, but this can hardly be considered authoritative.
2. *TRADITION*, Volume 11, No.4, Spring 1971, pp. 16–42.
2a. Goren, *Pesak Hadin Re: Inyan Ha'ach Vhaachot*, Jerusalem 5733, p. 137fl.
3. TRADITION, Volume 12, No. 3–4, Winter–Spring 1972, pp. 107–113.
4. Rabbi Yitzchak Greenberg, Mizrachi Fellowship Meeting, May 4, Fifth Avenue Synagogue.
5. B.T. *Yevamot* 46a.
6. *Ibid.*, 46b.
7. *Ibid.*, 47a.
8. *Mishneh Torah, Hilkhot Issurei Biah* 13:14–15.
9. *Ibid.*, 17.
10. B.T. *Bekhorot* 30b.
10a. B.T. *Yevamot* 47b.
11. *Ibid.*, 45b *Tosafot* ד"ה מי לא טבלה and also vide Ramban in his Novellae on *Yevamot* who comments on the statement of Rav Asi "Did she not bathe for the purpose of her menstruation," and insists upon acceptance of commandments.
12. *Yoreh Deah*, 268, 3. Vide *Iggerot Mosheh, Yoreh Deah*, 157, "Concerning the question as to whether a convert who has not accepted the commandments is considered a convert, it is simple and clear that he is not a convert at all even *post facto* . . ."
13. Maimonides, *Mishneh Torah, Hilkhot Issurei Biah*, 13, 4.
14. *Ibid.*, 14, 8.
15. This has nothing to do with the general disagreement amongst halakhic authorities as to whether or not the commandments require internal commitment, or *Kavannah*. The essence of the commandments here mentioned is their internal commitment, as explained by Rabbenu Yonah in B.T. *Berakhot*.
16. *Cf. Encyclopedia Talmudit*, Vol. 6, p. 431, note 80 where a similar distinction is suggested. Even the fact that Maimonides does not insist upon the informing of commandments for conversion *post facto* is not so clear. The *Yoreh Deah* re-words the *Mishneh Torah* as follows: "And if they did not investigate (the would–be convert as to his sincerity) or they did not inform him of the

reward of the commandments and their punishments . . ." he is still a convert (*Yoreh Deah*, 268, 13)." And perhaps this is an interpretation of the words of Maimonides himself: "A convert who they did not investigate or they did not inform of the commandments and their punishments . . ." but an informing of the contents of the commandments must take place. In any case, Maimonides does mention the acceptance of commandments as a procedure apart from the informing of commandments: "When the gentile is freed he requires another ritual immersion . . . but he does not require the acceptance of the commandments or to be informed the essentials of the religion." (*Mishneh Torah, Hilkhot, Issurei Biah*, 13, 12).

17. Vide Commentaries to Exodus 20:2, especially Ramban and Ibn Ezra, as well as Ramban, *Sefer Hamitzvot, Mitzvot Aseh* I, and Abarbanel, *Rosh Emanah.*

18. Cf. R. Chaim Ozer Grodzenski, *Achiezer* III, No. 26, sec. 4, and the discussion of that responsum by J. David Bleich, "The Conversion Crisis," TRADITION, VoL. 11, no. 4, Spring 1971, pp. 24–26.

19. *B.T. Yevamot.*

20. *Ibid.,* 109b, *Tosafot.*

21. *Yoreh Deah*, 268, 12 Vide *Shach* 23, "From Hillel it is to be learned that everything depends upon the evaluation of the court."

22. B.T. *Ketubot* 11a.

23. Rosh, *ad locum.*

24. *Yoreh Deah* 268, 7, 8.

25. It is interesting that Ritbah, quoted by the Shitah Mekubetset to B.T. *Ketuvot* 11a, asks about the lack of informing the minor as to the content of the commandments and concludes that since the minor cannot be properly informed, the conversion is still valid. The informing may not be necessary, but the acceptance certainly is.

26. Deuteronomy 6:5; *Sefer Hamitzvot of R.* Saadia Gaon, Positive Commandment 19.

27. R. I. Perlo, interpretation to *Sefer Hamitzvot* of R. Saadia Gaon, *Ibid.*

28. B.T. *Sanhedrin* 99b and B.T. *Yevamot* 109b, *Tosafot* ד"ה רעה

29. See note 21.

30. Vide *Encyclopedia Talmudit,* Vol. 6, p. 278, note 406.

31. Ruth 2:6.

32. *Ibid.,* 2: 10.

33. Cf. Genesis 12:1.

34. Ruth 2: 1 1, 12.

35. Isaiah 2:2–4.

36. Ruth 1:16, 17.

THE CONVERSION OF CHILDREN BORN TO GENTILE MOTHERS AND JEWISH FATHERS
J. Simcha Cohen

No rationale need be spelled out for a consideration of our topic. Current estimates are that one third of all marriages among American Jews involve a gentile partner, and few of them undergo a halakhically valid conversion. All halakhic authorities reject the notion of patrilineal descent, and the question naturally arises as to what our attitude should be toward Jewish men married to gentile women who want their children raised as Jews fully accepted by the halakhic community.

The key Talmudic text that deals with this issue is *Ketubot* 11a:

> R. Huna said: A minor proselyte is immersed by the knowledge of (*al da–at beit din*). What does this teach us? That it is an advantage for him [to be a Jew] and one may act for a person in his absence for his advantage. We have learned [this already]: One may act for a person in his absence for his advantage but one cannot act for a person in his absence for his disadvantage!
> [Here, though] you might have supposed that an idolator prefers a life without restraint (unbridled by Jewish law because it is established for us that a slave certainly prefers a dissolute life; therefore he (R. Huna) tells us that this is said [only in the case] of a grown up person who has already tasted sin, but [in the case] of a minor it is an advantage for him [to become a Jew].
> It seems that [the preceding Mishna] supports him (R. Huna). [It speaks of "a woman proselyte, a woman captive and a woman slave who have been redeemed, converted or freed (when they were less than three years and one day old)." Must they not have been immersed by the direction of *beit din*? No; here [the Mishna] treats the case of a proselyte whose sons and daughters were converted with him, so they are satisfied with what their father does.
>
> R. Yosef said: "When they come of age they can protest [against their conversion]"

A simple reading of the text is that a *beit din* may convert an infant gentile. The rationale is that being Jewish is considered a privilege, a *zekhut*, and one may confer an advantage upon a person even without his knowledge. This principle is recorded in the *Shulhan Arukh (Yoreh Deah* 268:7) as the authoritative halakhah.

Yet straightforward as the Talmudic text appears, this basic halakhic principle was not accepted universally at face value.

In 1864, Rabbi Bernard Illowy of New Orleans, a former student of the Hatam Sofer, ruled that sons born to Jewish fathers and gentile mothers could not be circumcised by a *mohel*. His rationale was that since such sons were not Jewish, the circumcision might cause people to mistakenly identify them as Jews. To solicit support for his halakhic position, R. llowy presented his case publicly in *Der Israelit* (an Orthodox Journal published in Germany), requesting the European Rabbinate to respond. Of major pertinence to us is the public exchange of views between Rabbi Zvi Hirsch Kalischer (1795–1894) and Rabbi Ezriel Hildesheimer (1820–1899). R. Kalischer permitted such a circumcision as well as the conversion of children born to gentile mothers, while R. Hildesheimer disputed his ruling and prohibited such conversions.[1]

R. Kalischer made the following comments regarding the Talmudic discussion in *Ketubot*: Rashi contended that R. Huna's dictum that the *beit din* may convert a minor relates to a case where the mother alone brought the child to *beit din* for conversion. The Talmudic text further contends that when the parents convert together with the child, R. Huna's dictum is not applicable. This seems to suggest that in the original instance the mother did not herself convert when she brought her child to *beit din* for a conversion. Even though the child would be reared subsequently by a gentile mother, R. Huna permitted the *beit din* to conduct the conversion. As such, concludes R. Kalischer, if a *beit din* may convert one who will be reared by a gentile mother, considering it a privilege (*zekhut*) for the child, so much more so when the child's father (a Jew) brings his son for conversion: the child wishes to emulate his father and we have good reason to expect the child to grow up Jewishly.

R. Hildesheimer retorted that we have no way of being certain that the gentile mother posited by Rashi intended to raise the child herself; perhaps either the child would be reared by observant Jews or it is known definitely that the gentile mother would rear the child according to the dictates of Torah and not *avodah zarah*. In the modern case of a gentile mother and Jewish father bringing their child to be converted, however, we cannot automatically apply R. Huna's principle.

In 1949, when Rabbi Yechiel Yaakov Weinberg (the last Rosh Yeshiva of the Hildesheimer Berlin Rabbinical Seminary) was asked his opinion in a case wherein a Jewish father and gentile mother brought their child to *beit din* for conversion, he did not focus on the argument as outlined here, but instead quoted the basic guideline which to this day serves as the pivotal negation of most child conversions:[2] The Talmud in *Ketubot* rules that a *beit din* has the authority to convert a child; this is because being a Jew is a privilege (*zekhut*) and one may confer a *zekhut* without another's knowledge. But to have a Jewish child grow up in a home that transgresses basic Jewish beliefs and observances is not deemed a *zekhut*, he said; it is rather a disadvantage and liability. Accordingly, a *beit din* has no authority to implement such a conversion. This guideline basically invalidates the legitimacy of the conversion of any child raised in a non–observant milieu. (indeed, this principle has a far–reaching effect in another social issue: adoption. Jewish families seeking to adopt children are faced with a number of obstacles. Should they attempt to adopt a Jewish child, rabbinic authorities require exact data about the parents of the child to mitigate concerns about illegitimacy;[3] frequently, the exact information is difficult to acquire. Accordingly, many people prefer to adopt a gentile child and convert the child during infancy. Yet, if the adopted parents of such a child are not themselves observant, a *beit din* may not convert the child.[4])

Though the argument mandating an observant familial milieu in order to validate a conversion may appear straightforward and logical, with all due respect and reverence, it seems that a fine reading of our text in *Ketubot* does not force such a conclusion. Consider the following questions:

1. Rashi notes that R. Huna's ruling relates to a situation in which the mother brought her child to a *beit din* for conversion, suggesting that had the father been present the legal process of conversion might have differed. But, what is the pragmatic halakhic distinction between a mother and a father in this matter?

2. R. Huna states "*Ger katan matbilin oto al da'at beit din* through the knowledge of *beit din*." The phrase "*al da 'at beit din*" connotes a special role for the court in the conversion of a child separate and distinct from its function during the conversion of an adult. What is this additional role?

3. Rashi states that "*beit din* becomes a surrogate father during the conversion of a child." Why is such a status necessary and what purpose does it serve?

4. The Talmud states that R. Huna's dictum may not be derived from the Mishna, as the Mishna refers to a case wherein the parents converted with the child. In that situation, the child is assumed to approve of the actions of his parents. Yet, the pragmatic distinction between the two cases is unclear. The implication is that R. Huna's case is an innovative role for *beit din*. What is that role?

5. A valid halakhic conversion requires four integral elements: *Kabbalat Mitsvot* (the awareness of and commitment to observe the commandments [5]); *Milah* (circumcision for a male convert); *Tevilah* (immersion in a *mikveh*); and *Beit Din* (the presence of a Rabbinical Court). Should anyone of these factors not be present, the conversion is not proper. A child certainly cannot (and does not) comprehend the meaning of *mitsvot* or the need for their observance; nor can he or she possess the ability to make a commitment to observe *mitsvot* in the future. As such, the entire conversion should be deemed invalid for it lacks the essential element of *kabbalat mitsvot*.

To resolve these difficulties it is necessary to posit a new frame of reference which sets guidelines for the discussion.

Shita Mekubbetset on our text poses the latter question regarding the lack of *kabbalat mitsvot* at the conversion of a child. He cites Ritva and *Shita Yeshana* who contend that *kabbalat mitsvot* is a vital element of the conversion process only in those cases where such commitment is physically possible to ascertain. In cases where the potential convert has the physical and intellectual capacity to be aware of *mitsvot* and make a commitment to observance, then and only then is this essential for a legal conversion. In such instances, the lack of *kabbalat mitsvot* would invalidate the conversion. For an infant or child, however, where *kabbalat mitsvot* is beyond the child's physical capability of comprehension, this element is deemed non–essential to the conversion process. In other words, any consideration of *mitsvot* is not germane to the validity of such a conversion. Consequently, R. Huna's rule and the Talmudic discussion do not make any reference to observance. Indeed, to infuse the concept of *kabbalat mitsvot* into our text is contrary to Ritva's position and a misreading of the discussion. The issue, it seems, concerns a completely different concept.

We suggest that the Talmud is concerned with the issue of *consent* and not observance. A *beit din* is not permitted to coerce anyone, adult or child, to involuntarily accept conversion. The process must be a voluntary one, accepted willingly by the potential convert. Should the conversion be coerced, then it is deemed invalid.[6]

The Talmud contends that R. Huna's principle is not applicable to a case in which parents convert together with their child. For in such a ease, "the child consents to [join] the action of his parents." In other words, an act which emulates the action of parents–the role models–is deemed implied consent to the conversion process. The conversion has legal standing even should one dispute R. Huna's principle, that *beit din* may convert a minor. R. Huna's case is different; he deals with a situation in which parents are not converting together with their child. In such a case, the problem of consent looms as a major issue. What authority does *beit din* have to convert a child without any concern as to whether there is consent to such a process? To this R. Huna innovates the concept that the conversion process is conferred "*al da 'at beit din.*" It is not the authority or power of *beit din* which is invoked, but rather *da'at*–knowledge, consent. That is, *beit din* affirms consent for the child, for being a Jew is a privilege, and one may confer a privilege upon another even without his or her knowledge. With *beit din* thus affirming consent for the child, the conversion is thereby presumed to be a voluntary process. This is the meaning behind Rashi's comment that the *beit din* becomes a surrogate father for the child; it becomes a surrogate parent for purposes of consent. Of interest is that this commentary of Rashi is cited by the *Beit Yosef* [*Yoreh De 'ah* 268] who notes that the *beit din* "becomes the father of the child who is converted through their hands." In other words, the court has a unique role to play in the conversion of a child distinct from that performed at the conversion of an adult. In the former case, they guarantee consent to legitimize the conversion.

Of concern are the particulars of the case in which R. Huna presents his principle. It is clear that R. Huna is not dealing with a situation where parents converted with the child. The *Tosefot Rid* [*Ketubot* 11a] suggests that R. Huna deals with a case of either an orphaned, destitute gentile youth or a child who was captured; the *Shita Mekubbetset* presents other options. Yet Rashi maintains that R. Huna is dealing with a case of a mother who brings the child to *beit din.* Indeed, it is Rashi's view that must be seriously considered above and beyond that of other authorities, for it is Rashi's position which is officially recorded in the Codes (see *Yoreh De'ah* 268:7).

The implication of Rashi's interpretation is that had the father brought the child to the *beit din*, R. Huna's principle would not be operational. Indeed, the Bah specifically notes that when the father brings the child for conversion, *da'at beit din* is not necessary.[7]

Rashi apparently is of the opinion that no proper conversion can occur without the precondition of consent. Just as a child who converts with his parents consents to performing a similar act, a father has the authority to grant consent to a *beit din* for the conversion of his child. The determination of the religion of the child is the father's prerogative. Consequently, when the father grants consent to convert his son, the *beit din* is not needed to utilize its good offices for consent.

There are two options for interpreting Rashi's position on the role of the mother:

> 1. Rashi believes that *beit din* has no authority to convert orphan children. *Beit din* cannot presume that the concept of *zekhut* is sufficient to imply consent. Consequently, only the wishes of a mother together with the concept of *zekhut* can enact a legitimate conversion.
>
> 2. Rashi feels that only a father and not a mother has the authority to grant consent; a mother's views are immaterial (see glosses of R. Yaakov Emden).

Regardless of which interpretation we accept, the specific language of the *Shulhan Arukh* supports our general position: If a gentile child has a father, the father may convert him; and if he does not have a father and (himself) seeks to be converted or his mother brings him to he converted, then *beit din* converts him, "for it is (deemed) an advantage to him (the child) and one may confer an advantage even without the beneficiary's presence" [*Yoreh De'ah* 268:7]. In the opening section, "the father may convert him." In the latter section (where the father is not present), "*beit din* converts him for it is a *zekhut*." The concept of *zekhut* is applicable only in the absence of a father bringing the child for conversion.

The text of the *Shulhan Arukh* forces us to understand that the entire aspect of *zekhut* is a material issue only when *beit din* must utilize the principle of *da'at beit din.* In such an instance, the consent of *beit din* is granted only when there is an assurance of observance of *mitsvot.* Otherwise, *beit din* does not authorize consent for the conversion. In an instance of a parent bringing his child to *beit din, da 'at beit din* is not necessary for the conversion. Parental consent is sufficient and it may even be deemed a complete *zekhut* without any consideration of *kabbalat mitsvot.* Fathers have personal rights over their children, and children consider it important to emulate their fathers. Observance of *mitsvot* in no way affects this principle. The *Shulhan Arukh* clearly notes a distinction between the cases and rules that the concepts of *zakhin* and *da'at beit din* are not applicable when a father brings his son for conversion.

The above analysis argues against R. Weinberg's halakhic challenge to the legitimacy of the conversion of children born to an irreligious Jewish father and a gentile mother, for in such an instance, the concept of *zekhut* is not germane. Indeed, since the conversion is valid without the principle of *zakhin* or *al da'at beit din*, any question as to whether it is in fact a *zekhut* or a liability is immaterial to the conversion process.

This suggests that the debate between R. Kalischer and R. Hildesheimer may have been more subtle than we thought.

R. Hildesheimer contended that R. Huna dealt with a case where either the mother gave the child to *beit din* to rear according to Torah values or it was certain that the gentile mother would insure that the child observed *mitsvot*. In other words, since according to Rashi and the *Shulhan Arukh* approval of the mother is not sufficient to provide consent for a conversion, and *beit din* must therefore use the principle of *zekhut*, then the mother's commitment for the child's observance is necessary for *beit din* to assume that the process is indeed a *zekhut* and not a liability. But if the father brings the child to *beit din*, no commitment for observance is necessary.

Parents cannot assume the commitment of *kabbalat mitsvot* for their children. The only reason parental consent may be necessary is to insure that the conversion was not coerced. To assume that the Talmud discusses a case where *beit din* assumes total responsibility for the child is simply far-fetched. Or, one may conjecture that since a gentile mother's commitment for observance is meaningless, *beit din* would not provide consent al *da 'at beit din* unless it also assumed responsibility to rear the child. Again, such extra precautions would only apply when the conversion was *al da 'at beit din*.

R. Kalischer contended that if the *beit din* could convert a child and return that child to the gentile mother's home, it certainly should permit a child of a gentile mother to be reared by a Jewish father. When a gentile mother alone brings her child to a *beit din*, the principle of *zakhin* is applicable. *Beit din* must then manifest concern that religious observance transpires so that no future disadvantage results. But when the father brings the child to *beit din*, the principle of *zakhin* is immaterial and, therefore, concern for observance is totally extraneous to the issue.

Now, what difference is there whether a gentile father or a Jewish father presents his child to *beit din* for conversion? To the extent that "consent" of a parent is all that is necessary in such a case, there should be no difference in law. The original proposal to have Jewish fathers present their non–Jewish children to *beit din* for conversion appears to be based upon solid halakhic grounds. Since, moreover, *kabbalat mitsvot* is not necessary in this instance, the procedure would be readily acceptable to even the most non–observant Jew.

One possible criticism must be noted. According to Halakhah, gentiles follow patrilineal descent while Jews observe matrilineal descent. This means that from a halakhic view, the Jewish father of a child born to a non–Jewish woman is not the halakhic father of the son. The Jewish father may not have the right to express "consent" for a child that is not his halakhic son.

This criticism suggests that a gentile father but not a Jewish father may grant consent. But consent is simply a *gilui da'at*, an expression of approval which must be elicited from the father of a child. Indeed, a child knows that a certain person is his father. To the child, there is no difference between a halakhic father or a biological father. The concern is basically who has responsibility to make decisions for the child. If the child is sick, for example, a parent has the authority to sign "consent" for an operation. In ancient times, perhaps only the father could exercise comparable authority. In our society, the biological father has legal jurisdiction over a child; he may make a decision for the child relating to life and death. He, therefore, should have the authority to assume consent on actions for purposes of conversion for his child. Indeed, many *aharonim* have accepted this line of reasoning.

Rabbi Moshe Schik also discussed the propriety of converting a child born to a Jewish father and a gentile mother. He cited *Tosefot Yom Tov* [Mishna *Ketubot*, 4:3, and *Kiddushin* 3:13] who rules that *beit din* should not convert gentile children. R. Schik suggested that *Tosefot Yom Tov* relates to a case of a Jewish father and gentile mother; since the male is not the halakhic parent of the child he has no authority to submit such a child to *beit din* for conversion. R. Schik disagreed with this position. He suggested, rather, that a court, *lekhath'ila* (*ab initio*), has no authority to convert gentile children, for the conversion process is a form of robbery from a gentile. To the extent that gentile children inherit their fathers, the conversion takes the child away from the family. As such, he reasons, the conversion is prohibited without parental permission. Yet, where parents consent, one may definitely convert the child.[8] At no time does he discuss any need for observance of *mitsvot*.

Rabbi David Hoffman briefly cited this responsum and added the comment that "since according to the law of the government this father has authority over his son, even though he is not a son according to *Din Torah*, it is not a form of theft. As such, perhaps even *lekhat'hila* one may convert the child, but certainly *bedi'aved* it is valid."[9]

Rabbi Avraham Yitshak HaKohen Kook also discussed this issue[10] He too maintained that even though a Jewish father is not the halakhic father of a son born to a gentile mother, he still has the authority to submit the child to *beit din* for conversion. He utilized *Ketubot* 11a as substantiation for this principle. There the Talmud implies, according to Rashi, that when parents convert with their children, such children consent to the process. The Talmud makes no distinction as to whether the father converted prior to the conversion of the children or whether the father and children simultaneously converted. If the former is correct, then once the father converted he is no longer a gentile, but a Jew, and is no longer the halakhic father of his son. However, he still has authority over his children to submit them to *beit din* for conversion. This proves, contends R. Kook, that even a Jewish father has authority over his non–halakhic son. R. Kook notes that such authority may not depend on biology but may relate to anyone who is responsible for the rearing of a child.

(In terms of *pesak*, however, R. Kook required that the gentile mother should not protest the conversion. In addition, he refused to sanction such a conversion where *kabbalat mitsvot* is lacking. Though he suggested that Tosafot, *Sanhedrin* 68b, imply that *kabbalat mitsvot* is not required for the conversion of a child, he still felt that it is wrong to convert a child in a milieu where there is no probable opportunity for *kabbalat mitsvot*. Of interest is that R. Kook does not discuss the text of the *Shulhan Arukh (Yoreh De'ah* 268:7) which grants the father authority to submit his child to *beit din* for conversion without utilizing the principle of *zekhut* or any consideration of observance. As the *Shulhan Arukh* is the standard code, its conclusions should be granted halakhic priority over those of other scholars.)

It is clear that the requirement of "consent" is simply a means of preventing an involuntary conversion. It has nothing to do with a commitment to observe *mitsvot*. For this reason R. Yosef rules in our Talmudic text that upon maturity, such children converted during youth or infancy have an opportunity to renounce the conversion. Since such forms of conversion lack *kabbalat mitsvot*, the children are yet granted an opportunity to engage in this essential factor. This means that *kabbalat mitsvot* becomes necessary only when children have the capacity for such a commitment. Prior to maturity, a renunciation is not halakhically acceptable and upon the age of maturity the child is assumed to be automatically Jewish. When does the child have the opportunity to manifest either rejection or acceptance of his religious status?

Three options to express renunciation are presented by *Shita Mekubbetset* to our text in *Ketubot*.

> 1. Tosafot contend that upon the age of maturity the child is informed about the need to observe *mitsvot*. Should the child reject commitment, then he loses his Jewishness.
> 2. Ritva contends that R. Yosef speaks of a youngster who as a minor renounced his Jewishness, protesting his or her status as a Jew. Should this rejection persist until after the age of maturity, the child's conversion is invalidated.
> 3. Rosh notes that the child is observed at age of maturity. Should he observe Jewish customs, then he is deemed Jewish. Should he not be observant, his status is invalidated.[11]

Kabbalat mitsvot may not be essential or even germane to the conversion of a child, but it is vital to the ultimate status of such a convert. *Beit din* is not absolved from its obligations upon the formal conclusion of the rituals performed in youth. It must convene at the child's age of maturity to assess the status of the convert. For this reason Tosafot note that the child must be informed of the need to observe *mitsvot*. That is, *beit din* must convene and formally request *kabbalat mitsvot*. This procedure is a formal "act of *beit din*."

It is apparent that Ritva does not require a formal act of *beit din* to extract a commitment of *kabbalat mitsvot*. According to Ritva, the child retains his Jewishness as long as he does not reject it as a youth and persist in his rejection till maturity. This suggests that the concern has nothing to do with *kabbalat mitsvot*. Ritva does not require any assessment of observance. This may be due to his theory that once *kabbalat mitsvot* is not feasible (e.g., at the conversion of an infant), the entire concern for *kabbalat mitsvot* is never material to that particular conversion. The concern is, rather, one of "consent." For this reason as long as the child does not reject his Jewish status, the "consent" factor is implied and the child retains his Jewishness till maturity.

The position of Rosh is that *kabbalat mitsvot* is immaterial to the conversion of a child only because the child is unable to make such a commitment. This merely temporarily withholds such a requirement till a date when the commitment is physically and legally able to be assessed. Yet, no formal convening or *beit din* or *kabbalat mitsvot* is necessary. As long as the child is observed to follow Jewish customs, it is deemed sufficient to legitimize the conversion.

Hatam Sofer cites numerous opinions, including that of Bahag, who contend that if parents bring their child to *beit din* for conversion, even though the parents themselves do not convert, the child may not subsequently renounce the conversion, for the parents "accept the condition of the conversion for him."[12] The subsequent need of *kabbalat mitsvot* is nonessential. Once consent is provided for the conversion, it remains valid even without a subsequent *kabbalat mitsvot*.

In 1934, Rabbi Hayyim Ozer Grodzinski modified the above *pesak* of Hatam Sofer by contending that only children who are reared as observant Jews may not subsequently renounce their Jewish status. However, if during minority they violated Jewish law, then they retain the option of renunciation. But violation of Halakhah alone is not tantamount to renunciation; a formal renunciation is required. Though he felt that a *beit din* should preferably not be involved in such cases, he explicitly suggested that the rabbis should not publicly "storm" against such conversions and denigrate them, for according to Halakhah the conversions are valid. [13]

Whatever the final rule on the renunciation process, it is a problem to be resolved within the halakhic community as to the most desirable or practical, pragmatic procedure. This concern in no way invalidates or questions the principle that a Jewish father may legally convert his offspring from a gentile mother. Logic, moreover, could extend this concept to permit a non–observant Jewish father to halakhically convert an adopted gentile child. Since the concern is not for the observance of *mitsvot*, but rather for consent, even a non–biological father who is a surrogate father as a result of state law and responsible for the rearing of the child should have the halakhic authority to grant "consent" to a conversion.

Coupled with the above analysis there is another principle that sharply mitigates the charge that to be reared in a non–observant home is a liability and not a *zekhut*.

Rabbi David Halevi Horowitz, a distinguished scion of a Rabbinic family and Rav of Stanislav (1862–1935), was posed, in 1930, the exact question discussed herein by his son, Rabbi Moshe Halevi Horowitz of Vienna. The case involved a man who had married a gentile woman through the civil courts and subsequently had a son. A scholar forbade the couple to circumcise or convert the child. The rationale was that it is not a *zekhut* or advantage but a distinct disadvantage for a child to be reared in a non–observant home. Accordingly, any conversion would be invalid. R. Horowitz disagreed, maintaining that *beit din* had a *mitsvah*, an obligation, to perform the conversion. The contention that probable future nonobservance disqualifies the *zekhut* of the present and therefore invalidates the process was discounted for the following reasons:

1. Since the *Shulhan Arukh* and early commentaries did not mention such a concern, we should not presume to be wiser (or more cautious) than they.

2. The Talmud states (*Rosh Hashana* 16b) that a person is judged according to his deeds at the moment. (Rashi notes that this is applicable to a person who will eventually do evil.) Substantiation is the verse that "God has heard the voice of the lad there where he is" (*ba–asher hu sham*; Genesis 21: 17 and Rashi's commentary). Thus, even though Ishmael was subsequently to pillage and murder, he was still saved, for God judges each person at the moment of prayer without a view towards what will be in the future. This principle teaches us that a future disadvantage or liability does not invalidate the present. Indeed, to discount the present due to the future is a violation of this concept.

3. Every man may yet do *teshuvah*.

4. The *zekhut* of circumcision cannot be denied because of future transgressions. The Talmud notes that circumcision is great in that it is blessed with thirteen covenants [*Nedarim* 31b]. This *zekhut* is not to be discounted.[14]

Thus the concern that non–observance invalidates the *zekhut* of being a Jew is negated as an innovative apprehension not supported by Halakhah.

Support for the position that qualms over a child's future observance of *mitsvot* do not invalidate the halakhic status of a conversion may be derived from Tosafot, *Ketubot* 11a. Tosafot discuss the propriety of utilizing the concept of "*zakhin le–adam she–lo be–fanav* (acting for a person in his absence to his advantage)" to validate the conversion of a gentile child. They suggest that the principle of *zakhin* is deemed rabbinic in nature only in cases where a probable liability may occur. One may, therefore, not utilize *zakhin* to set aside *terumah* on behalf of another person, for any allocation above the bare minimum may be more or less in amount than the other wished to allocate, and the action may therefore entail a potential liability. In the case of a conversion, however, which is a complete advantage (*zekhut gamur*) the concept of *zakhin* may be applied even from a Biblical perspective. (This means that children converted by a *beit din* are classified as complete Jews even according to biblical law.)

This response requires clarification as to why the case of *terumah* is deemed a liability and that of conversion classified as a clear *zekhut*. It is possible that a person may subsequently express approval for any *terumah* allocations made on his behalf. At the same time, it is also possible that he may reject such actions. Does not the ease of conversion also contain these potential dual, contrary reactions? The child may subsequently either renounce the conversion or accept it willingly. Where is the distinction? A suggested solution is that the principle of *zakhin* does not relate to subsequent reactions or considerations. It deals with the psychological state of mind at the very moment of the action considered. At the moment a certain quantity of *terumah* is set aside, it is conceivable that one may consider such quantity excessive and therefore not approve of the action. This possible consideration of a liability at the moment of action (setting aside *terumah*) is sufficient to declassify it from a biblical viewpoint from being a complete *zekhut*.

At a conversion, however, there is no conceivable liability at the very moment of the conversion itself. A potential, subsequent rejection of the process does not enter into the considerations at the moment of conversion. Children have no liability in becoming Jewish, especially infant children. Since at the moment of conversion no liability exists, conversion is therefore deemed a complete advantage.

Thus according to Tosafot qualms over the irreligious milieu of a child convert cannot and should not invalidate the *zekhut* of the conversion even when *beit din* utilizes the concept of zakhin. To an infant child, at the moment of conversion the religious observance or non–observance of parents is immaterial. Accordingly, a future liability should not invalidate a clear, present *zekhut*. [15]

The issue of converting children born to gentile mothers has, of course, been treated by contemporary *posekim*.[16] Of special interest is the position of *gedol doreinu*, Hagaon Rav Moshe Feinstein,[17] of blessed memory. This writer some time ago sent a draft of this paper to R. Feinstein for his comments and criticism. His grandson, Rabbi Mordechai Tendler, who acted as his assistant and spokesman, wrote a response, dated Rosh Hodesh Kislev 5746 (November 14, 1985), in which he stated:

> Though within your *pilpul* there are items [with which], perhaps, we do not agree, the basic approach is apparent to us and on numerous occasions we have so ruled. Yet in all cases we try, whenever it is possible, to set up arrangements for the observance of *mitsvot*. [That is] that the parents should agree to provide a Jewish education for the child, or that they should agree to eat only kosher [food] in the home, or that they will not violate Shabbat publicly or all [these conditions]. This orientation was noted by *mori u–zekeni*, in his responsum [*Iggerot Moshe*] *Yoreh De'ah*, Part I, No. 158.
>
> Concerning an adopted child, it is not so simple to consider one who rears him to be like a father in this matter according to Din, but most likely such is the case.[18]

More recently, R. Feinstein's last volume of *Iggerot Moshe* included a responsum to teachers at a day school where a substantial number of the students had gentile mothers who had not been properly converted. His advice was to convert the children:

> They do not need *kabbalai mitsvot* and can be converted *al da'at beit din*. It is a *zekhut* for them; inasmuch as they are learning in a religious school under the tutelage of pious teachers, they will probably grow up to be *shomerei Torah*; while this is not certain, it is certainly a *zekhut*. And even if they do not grow up to be *shomerei* Torah, it seems logical that it is still a *zekhut*, as even Jewish sinners have Kedushat Yisrael–the *mitsvot* that they do are *mitsvot*,

and their sins are to them unintentional, Thus they have a greater *zekhut* than being gentiles.[19]

Orthodox Jewry is becoming a fortress separated from the general Jewish community. We feel it should not simply write off vast numbers of transgressors as outcasts. As long as Halakhah provides a device to properly convert children of intermarriage, this device should be utilized aggressively to make contact with vast numbers of Jews. It is an opportunity to crystallize rabbinic initiative and leadership. Should, for example, the *beit din* require a day school education as the essential requirement for conversion, then such children, at least, have a probable chance of becoming true Torah Jews. A public policy of conversion before a proper *beit din* places the process of conversion exactly where it should be: in the sphere of competent *benei Torah* knowledgeable of Halakhah.

Our concern is not to suggest authoritative halakhic policy on either side of the issue. It is, rather, to present an option that requires the forum of halakhic dialogue by scholars. We hope that this discussion will serve as a frame of reference for the decision.

NOTES

1. R. Howy's call was published in *Der Israelit*, 1864, No. 52. R. Hildeshcimer's position was published in *Der Israelit*. 1865, No.5. In the same year. R. Kalischer wrote a personal responsum to R. Hildesheimer concerning this issue. In the *Festschrift zum vierzigjahrigen Amtsjubilaum des Herrn Rabbiner Dr. Salomon Carlbach in Lubeck* (July 16, 1910), Dr. Meier Hildesheimer brought as his contribution to the volume a correspondence between his father Dr. Ezriel Hildesheimer and R. Hirsch Kalischer of Thorn. This exchange was subsequently included in the Responsa of R. Ezriel Hildesheimer, Nos. 229, 230 (London, 1969].

Each of the disputants was a great Torah scholar. R. Kalischer was internationally known as a harbinger of the Zionist idea. Though his most famous work, *Derishat Tsiyyon*, was an attempt to legitimize Zionist concerns within the religious community, he also published two major halakhic volumes entitled *Even Bohan* and *Moznayim la–Mishpat*. He was the rabbi of Thorn and as a youth he was a disciple of two universally acclaimed masters of Halakhah: R. Akiva Eiger of Posen and R. Yaakov of Lissa (Lorberbaum). R. Hildesheimer was the Rav of the Adas Yisrael Orthodox Congregation of Berlin. In 1873 he established a Rabbinical Seminary of which he was Rosh ha–Yeshiva. This yeshiva became a central institution for the training of Orthodox rabbis in Europe. As a youth he studied under R. Yaakov Ettlinger of Altona, the acclaimed scholarly author of the *Arukh la–Ner* commentaries on Talmud.

2. *Seridei Esh*. Vol. 11, Yoreh De'ah, Responsa, 95–96.
3. See *Iggerot Moshe, Yoreh De'ah*. No. 162; also R. Yosef Henkin, *Hapardes*. Sept. 1965. p. 7.
4. Dayan Yitshak Yaakov Weiss, Responsa *Minhat Yitshak*. Vol. III, No. 99.
5. See R. Shlomo Kluger [Responsa *Tuv Ta'am va–Da'at*. Vol. 2, III] who rules that *kabbalat mitsvot* without *milah* and *tevilah* is meaningless. Yet, *milah* and *tevilah* even without a prior *kabbalat mitsvot* is sufficient to validate the conversion from a Biblical viewpoint. Indeed, he notes that the requirement of *kabbalat mitsvot* prior to other rituals is but a Rabbinic law.
6. Bah, *Tur, Yoreh De'ah*, 268.
7. *Tur, Yoreh De'ah*, 268.
8. Responsa Maharam Schik, Vol. II, *Yoreh De'ah* 248.
9. Responsa *Melammed le–Ho'il. Yoreh De'ah* 87.
10. Responsa *Da'at Kohen*, Nos. 147–148.
11. See *Arukh ha–Shulhan, Yoreh De'ah* 268:13, who cites all three theories.
12. Responsa *Hatam Sofer, Yoreh De'ah* 253.
13. Responsa *Ahiezer*, Part III, No. 28.

One scholar suggests that when a Jewish father brings his child (born to a gentile mother) to *beit din* for conversion, subsequent renunciation of the conversion is not permitted. His rationale is as follows:

Rambam permits Jewish soldiers during a war, under certain circumstances to have sexual relations with gentile women (*Hilkhot Melakhim* 8:1). Such women, moreover, are granted an option to convert to Judaism and remain as wives of their Jewish husbands (*ibid.*, 8:5). In the event that such women refuse to convert, they have permission to remain in Jewish households for a maximum of twelve months (*ibid.*. 8:7). Should one such woman become pregnant as a result of her original sexual encounter with the Jewish soldier, *beit din* may convert the child while he is yet a minor (*ibid.*, 8:8). *Kesef Mishneh* notes that this is based on R. Huna's dictum permitting *beit din* to convert minor children (*Ketubot* 11a). It is important to note that Rambam makes no reference to the option of renunciation when the child matures. (See *ibid.*, 10:3, where Rambam rules that a minor convert may renounce the conversion upon maturity.) Indeed, even scholars who contend that when parents convert together with their children the option of renunciation is not applicable, do not cite this ruling of the Rambam (*ibid.*, 8:8). The distinction may he that when a Jewish father brings his child to *beit din*, such a child has "part Jewish blood" in his lineage, and no renunciation is permitted (Responsa R. Avraham Moshe Fingerhut No. 16 [former head, *Beit Din* Paris, Jerusalem 1963].

It should also he noted that R. Meir Simcha of Dvinsk rules that parents have an inherent right to convert minor children because they sustain and support the children's existence (*Meshekh Hokhmah. Parashat Bo*). Therefore, reasons R. Shmuel Katz, *Av Beit Din*, Rabbinical Council of Southern California, such children may not subsequently renounce their conversion upon maturity. Renunciation is an option only when conversion occurs through the principle of *zakhin*. In an instance, however, where a father brings his son to *beit din* for conversion, such a concept is not applicable. The authority for the conversion is the inherent right given to parents who sustain children [*Devar Shemuel*, Responsum I, 1986].
14. Responsa, *Imrei David*. 172b.

Imrei David's ruling that present actions should not be disqualified because of premonitions over future observance may be bolstered by the following:

> The Talmud (*Berakhot* 10a) records that King Hezekiah was informed by the prophet, "Set thy house in order, for thou shalt die and not live" [Isaiah 38: I]. What is the meaning of "thou shalt die and not live?" Thou shalt die in this world and not live in the world to come. He [Hezekiah] said to him, "why so bad?" [Isaiah] replied, "Because you did not try to have children." He said, "The reason was that I saw by the Holy Spirit that the children issuing from me would not be virtuous. "[Isaiah] said to him, "What have you to do with the secrets of the All–Merciful" You should have done what you were commanded, and let the Holy One, Blessed be He, do that which pleases Him."

From this we derive the rule that man must strive to do a *mitsvah* even though the future result may be ominous. Man's role is to observe a present *mitsvah* and not detract from such observance due to premonitions over the future. The same applies to the conversion of a child. Its present status of a *mitsvah* may not be disqualified because of qualms over probable future observance. The commentators contend that although Hezekiah's children may be evil, his children's children may yet be righteous [See *Iyyun Yaakov, Ein Yaakov, Berakhot* 10a]. Similarly, a convert may grow up in an irreligious home but feel pride in his Jewishness. He, or even his child's child, may yet return to Torah. The "Baal Teshuvah" movement throughout the world substantiates this concept.
15. This explanation challenges the position of Rabbi J. David Bleich that the Talmud itself negates the validity of child converts reared by unobservant parents. His argument is as follows:

Referring to our Talmudic text, R. Bleich suggests that should one conceive of a situation wherein sin took place, then it is evident that the conversion is not a *zekhut*. A child reared in an irreligious home certainly tasted sin and should be comparable to a slave who prefers a dissolute life.

Yet, even this objection R. Bleich counters by noting the position of Tosafot, *Sanhedrin* 68b, that the *ger* converts himself and does not need the principle of *zakhin*. Accordingly, the fact that the conversion is not a complete *zekhut* should not invalidate the process [*Hapardes*" Vol 58, No.2, Nov. 1983, pp. 17–19].

This position simply may not be derived from the text.

A. The Talmud in *Ketubot deals* with minor children, including a child of seven or ten years of age. (Indeed, the *Shulhan Arukh* [*Yoreh De'ah* 268:7] rules that R. Huna's dictum relates to children who come to *beit din* by themselves.) Such children have been reared in a gentile home prior to conversion. They have not observed commandments prior to conversion. They could conceivably be described as "living in sin." Yet, the Talmud still makes the distinction between a minor and an adult. It says a minor has "not tasted sin"; namely, a minor's experience with sin is not equal to that of an adult. His judgment valuing sin over commandments is not granted validity.

The fact that all minor children regardless of age are acceptable for conversion, clearly indicates that the milieu of the child convert has no bearing on the legitimacy of the conversion.

B. Just as the past of the child has no negative overtones, neither does the future. R. Huna is concerned only with the psychological state at the moment of conversion. The fact that the child may subsequently renounce the conversion does not retroactively invalidate the conversion while he is still a minor. The *zekhut* of conversion relates only to the conditions at the time of the conversion. Since all children are deemed to be in a state of innocence, the conversion is considered a complete *zekhut*.

Rabbi Elya Pruzhiner notes that the principle of *zakhin* has legal standing for a minor only if at the moment utilized there is a clear privilege accruing to the minor [*Halikhot Eliyahu*, Part I, *Even ha–Ezer*, 33). R. Pruzhiner's theory has been erroneously cited as specifically relating to conversion, i.e., that the privilege must be evident at the time of conversion and not be based upon the possibility thereof in the future. [See R. Melech Schachter, "Various Aspects of Adoption," *Journal of Halakha and Contemporary Society*, Vol IV, Fall 1982, p.101; he cites ch. 31.1 *Halikhot Eliyahu* articulated a general rule and never explicitly related it to conversion. Indeed, as noted, the halakhic status of innocence of a minor deems all actions on his behalf as a complete *zekhut* at the time of conversion.

16. Rabbi Shelomo Goren in his capacity as Chief Rabbi of Israel, ruled that *beit din* may convert the minor child of a Jewish father even in an instance where the mother does not convert herself and remains a gentile. He, moreover, openly declared that *kabbalat mitsvot* is not applicable in the conversion of a minor. In the event that *tevilah* must be postponed to a date subsequent to the circumcision (e.g., for an infant) he maintained that such a child should be registered in Israel as "*mityahed*" (becoming Jewish). However, when all rituals are completed, such a child may be registered as a full–fledged Jew ["*Efsharuyot le–Gerut shel Ketanim*," *Shana be–Shana*, 5744, pp. 151–155]. At no time does R. Goren even suggest that the conversion may be invalidated because of the status of the mother or the irreligious milieu of the family. This appears to corroborate the thesis presented.

17. See *Iggerot Moshe, Yoreh De'ah*, Vol. I, No. 158, where R. Feinstein rules:

1. The concept of *zakhin* is not applicable when a father brings his son to *beit din* for conversion.

2. A Jewish father may bring his child born to a gentile mother to *beit din* for conversion. Even though such a person is not the halakhic father, he yet has the authority to convert his child.

R. Feinstein also adds a nuance of pragmatic importance relating to the conversion of children. He suggests that it would be proper (*nakhon hadavar*) to re–immerse child converts in a *mikveh* when they reach maturity. Why? In our country it is not so certain, he writes, that conversions of children are a complete *zekhut* since it is probable that the children will not observe *Shabbat* and may violate other prohibitions. Notwithstanding such concerns, the conversion is still a *zekhut*, for Jewish sinners are deemed better than gentiles. In addition, perhaps the *zekhut* is simply the fact that a child consents to do that which his father requests. Also, when the mother converts, the *zekhut* is complete. As such, it is probable that the conversion of children is, indeed, a *zekhut*. Yet, to eliminate any qualms over the matter, it is advisable to re–immerse the child at maturity.

18. To insure that the contents were fully understood, I called Rabbi Mordechai Tendler to review the letter. I noted that he used the phrase "*anu mishtadlin* (we try)" to acquire a commitment for *mitsvot* and questioned him as to the halakhah should such endeavors be impossible to achieve. His response was. "We do not invalidate the conversion."

19. [*Iggerot Moshe. Even ha–Ezer*, Vol. 4, Responsum 26].

BURIAL OF NON–HALAKHIC CONVERTS
Moshe J. Yeres

I

The significance of a Jewish cemetery as sacred ground reserved solely for the burial of Jews is well documented in Jewish tradition and history. So important was this requirement, and so universal was its acceptance, that the first purchase of property by Jewish communities of the Diaspora was usually for a tract of cemetery land. This often preceded even the acquisition of a building or land for a permanent synagogue structure.[1] The sanctity of the Jewish cemetery was formalized by the erection of a wall or fence which quite rigidly conferred the boundaries of the *beit ha–kevarot*.[2] Its special sanctity–*kedushat beit ha–kevarot*–extended to the entire tract of land within those boundaries.[3]

This law that Jews, and only Jews, are to be buried in a specifically Jewish cemetery–is often taken for granted. The Rabbis understood it to be operable even as early as the First Temple period. The *Targum* to Ruth I: 17 interprets the statement *ba–asher tamuti amut ve–sham ekaver–*"where thou diest will I die, and there will I be buried"–as a recognition by Ruth that her conversion to Judaism will allow her the privilege of being buried in a Jewish cemetery, a privilege clearly understood to be reserved solely for members of the Jewish faith.[4]

The Talmud makes no direct reference to this halakhah. In fact, the Talmud in *Gittin* 61a seems to imply the opposite when it quotes a *baraita* which states *ve–koverin metei nokhrim im metei Yisra‘el mipeni darkhei shalom*, "we bury the dead of the heathen along with the dead of Israel in the interests of peace." However, Rashi very clearly explains that this does not mean that they are to be buried together in the same cemetery:

> Along with the dead of Israel: [This does] not [mean that the non–Jewish dead are buried] in a Jewish cemetery, but rather that we take care of their [funeral arrangements] if the non–Jewish dead are found slain together with the Jewish dead[5]

This explanation is repeated by a number of Rishonim, all of whom assume that it is unthinkable under any circumstance to inter non–Jews in the same cemetery as Jews.[6] *Bah*, however, does interpret the *baraita's* statement to allow for the actual burial of non–Jewish deceased alongside the Jewish deceased:

> However. . . [the Talmud's statement in *Gittin* 61a] comes to teach us that

they can bury the [non–Jewish] dead in a Jewish cemetery if the bodies were found slain together with Jewish bodies. And even though we never bury a non–Jew next to a Jew. . . however [in this case] since the bodies were discovered slain together, he can bury the non–Jewish deceased in the same courtyard as the Jewish deceased, because of *darkhei shalom*.[7]

Yet *Bah* makes it quite clear that the Talmud's case is the sole exception to what is otherwise an unbending prohibition to inter non–Jews in a Jewish cemetery. Furthermore, it has been argued that even *Bah* did not intend to allow the positioning of non–Jewish graves immediately adjoining Jewish graves; rather his permission was limited to *hatser ehad*–burial within "the same courtyard."[8] In short, it has always been an accepted fact within Jewish tradition that Jews and only Jews have the privilege of burial within the sacred confines of the Jewish cemetery.[9]

II

The exclusiveness of Jewish cemetery ground, reserved solely for Jews, generally continued unquestioned even into the Modern era. However, together with the twin inroads of emancipation and assimilation, there now arose the very real issue of intermarried (mixed marriage) couples, and their desire to be buried together after death, just as they had lived together in life. The Jewish partner of such mixed marriages, despite his or her having married outside the faith, still coveted the privilege of burial in the Jewish cemetery. That he or she remained eligible for such burial privileges never seems to have been contested in the responsa; the only proviso discussed is that the Jewish partner of such a marriage not be buried next to the graves of righteous and religious Jews, but rather somewhat removed from them. This is similar to the Halakhah's approach to the burial of apostates and others who have rebelled against basic Jewish tenets.[10]

The issue appears to have been first dealt with by R. Hayyim Palache who refers to an actual case where the Jewish partner of a mixed marriage was buried in the Jewish cemetery, in an area somewhat removed from the other graves.[11] R. Jekutiel Judah Greenwald best summarizes the halakhic stance when he writes in *Kol Bo al Avelut*:

Regarding the [Jewish] man married to a non–Jewish woman. . . or the [Jewish] woman married to a non–Jewish man. . . who died. . . since [the law is that] we are obligated to bury even complete sinners in a Jewish cemetery, surely we are obligated to bury these. However, they ought not to be buried among [the graves of] religious Jews, rather among [the graves of] those of similar [Jewish religious character].[12]

III

On the other hand, the non–Jewish partner of a mixed marriage or the children of a non–Jewish wife[13] could not be eligible for burial rights in the Jewish cemetery because they were not Jewish. Or so it should have been obvious. However, in the Modern era, this question has been raised a number of times, as Jews who have married outside the faith have requested and at times demanded that their non–Jewish spouses be buried alongside them,[14] and that their children from a non–Jewish wife be buried in the Jewish cemetery because of their Jewish paternity. [15]

One such incident is well recorded. In 1903, the Jewish cemetery in Temesvar (Timisoara), Hungary allowed the burial of a five–year old boy from a non–Jewish mother. Immediately Rabbi Bernat Schück of Temesvar took up the cudgels against this unconscionable anti–halakhie act. Rabbi Schück wrote to the leading Orthodox rabbis and scholars of his day asking for their support in his opposition to the cemetery's action, and for their advice on his proposed secession from that cemetery and his formation of an independent Orthodox *hevra kaddisha* and cemetery grounds. Many rabbis responded to his letter, and the wealth of polemic writings was collected and published by Rabbi Schück in a booklet entitled *Dat ve–Din, Hit es Allam*.[16] Among those who responded was Rabbi David Tzvi Hoffmann. He concurred with Rabbi Schück, that this wanton act–the burial in a Jewish cemetery of the offspring of a non–Jewish mother should not be condoned by the local Orthodox community, and that Rabbi Schück ought to secede and form his own cemetery.[17]

Another who dealt with this type of question was R. Hayyim Eleazar Shapira, the author of *Minhat Elazar*, who prohibited a Jewish cemetery from accepting for burial the son of a Jewish father and a non–Jewish mother. In this case, though the child had been circumcised, the circumcision was not done *le–shem gerut*, and the child was therefore not considered Jewish.[18] In the last century, the question of Jewish burial rights for non–Jewish marriage partners and the children of non–Jewish wives has been posed numerous times to halakhie authorities; [19] though interestingly enough, even those who posed the questions never argued with the fact that these people were clearly not considered Jewish according to Halakhah.

R. Moshe Feinstein was asked how to deal with this situation in a case where the accepted procedure within a Jewish cemetery had been to bury non–Jews next to their Jewish spouses. Rabbi Feinstein responded that the area where all other Jews are buried[20] must be separated from the "mixed" area where these Jewish and non–Jewish marriage partners are buried, by a space of eight *amot* (cubits) plus a fence no less than ten *tefahim* (handbreadths) high.[21] Rabbi Feinstein makes it clear that these requirements of separation apply not only for the burial of religiously observant Jews (*"shomerei Torah"*) in that cemetery, but for any Jew who wishes to be buried there in accordance with *"dinei Yisra 'el"*; the criterion for separation is the *"kedushat Yisra'el"* of the deceased.[22] Other *posekim* have prohibited the burial of a non–Jewish spouse in a Jewish cemetery even if there is the separation of a fence from the other Jewish graves.[23]

IV

The above rulings appear clear–cut and simple. However, we now discuss applying this to a non–halakhic convert to Judaism, that is to say, a conversion performed *she–lo ka–halakhah*, by a non–Orthodox rabbi.[24] We obviously work with the premise that such a non–halakhic conversion does not effect any change in the religious status of the individual; he or she is still considered not Jewish.[25] But with regard to burial in a Jewish cemetery, do the same strictures apply as with a complete non–Jew, as indeed this non–halakhic convert does not possess *kedushat Yisra'el*;[26] or may limited privileges of burial in a Jewish cemetery be extended at times to one who does not meet the strict requirements of *kedushat Yisra'el*?

This is a very significant issue, for today's Orthodox rabbi is often called on to officiate at funerals where the interment takes place at cemeteries controlled by independent lodges and "benefit" organizations. As such, the religious status of those accepted for burial in these cemeteries is not under the control of the local Orthodox rabbinate. And while many of these lodges and "benefit" cemeteries do not permit the burial of blatant non–Jews (even where the other marriage partner is Jewish), they will accept for burial privileges any convert to Judaism regardless of whether the conversion was performed by an Orthodox rabbi *ka–halakhah* or by a Conservative or Reform rabbi *she–lo ka–halakhah*.[27] In such cemeteries it is therefore more than likely to find non–halakhic converts buried. The questions then become: how would this impinge upon the burial of other Jews in such a cemetery, both religiously observant Jews and the non–observant; how ought an Orthodox rabbi respond to a request to officiate at an interment in this type of cemetery; and how careful does a cemetery actually need to be in ascertaining that those Jews (and specifically converts to Judaism) accepted for burial privileges have the status of halakhic *kedushat Yisra'el*?

Historically, this issue was discussed long before Reform and Conservative conversion practices arose which deviated from the Halakhah. In a case reported by R. Abraham 1. Gatigno in *Tseror ha–Kesef,* a gentile maid–servant (*shifhah*) who became ill requested of her Jewish master to be converted to Judaism. She did not recover; and though she passed away after undergoing *kabbalat hamitsvot* in the presence of a *beit din*, she had not yet undergone immersion in a *mikveh*. As a result, her conversion remained incomplete. Nonetheless, her body was allowed to be buried in the Jewish cemetery ("*tokh kivrei Yisra'el* "). Though she had obviously not acquired *kedushat Yisra'el*, not having undergone *tevilah*, she was still accorded Jewish burial privileges.[28] In a similar case where the maid–servant of a Jew had begun to carry out certain *mitsvot*, but had not formally undergone *kabbalat ha–mitsvot* or *tevilah* in the presence of a *beit din* (though she had undergone *tevilah le–shem gerut* in the presence of her owner's mother), R. Elijah b. Benjamin Halevi did not require that her body once buried be disinterred from the Jewish cemetery; however, it is possible that had he been consulted prior to the actual burial, he might have decided diffcrently.[29]

R. Hayyim Eleazar Shapira, discussing in Responsa *Minhat Elazar* the prohibition of accepting for Jewish burial the child of a non–Jewish mother,[30] raises *inter alia* the question of a non–Jew who underwent circumcision *le–shem gerut* but died prior to the *tevilah*. R. Shapira felt that in this case it would only be logical to allow burial in a Jewish cemetery.[31] As to whether a distance of eight *amot* is needed to separate such a grave from other Jewish graves, R. Shapira does not reach a definite conclusion.[32]

In all of these cases there was no completed *gerut*; yet the deceased was accepted for burial in the Jewish cemetery. It appears, then, that the criterion of personal status for burial may not always be the same as for other issues of Jewish personal status, such as marriage. For surely we would not permit an incomplete *ger* or even a questionable *ger* to marry a Jew simply because he or she had strong intentions to identify with Judaism. However, in the cases discussed above, though the deceased had not been formally admitted to the Jewish community, his or her will to identify with the Jewish community and with Judaism is considered sufficient to allow for Jewish burial privileges. Though the deceased had not undergone a full and complete conversion to Judaism and obviously did not meet the strict halakhic requirements for *kedushat Yisra'el*, his or her decision to identify with Halakhic Judaism is sufficient to permit burial in a Jewish cemetery.

A related question is discussed by a nineteenth–century Orthodox rabbi and scholar in the United States, Rabbi Bernard Illowy. The case concerned a convert to Judaism who died in 1856 in Nashville, Tennessee, and was buried in the Jewish cemetery. Her husband, however, was unable to produce a certificate attesting to the halakhic validity of the conversion, and, as a result, questions and doubts were raised. R. Illowy allowed the woman's body to remain buried based on the *hazakah* that until now she was considered Jewish, and especially since, in this case, she had clearly observed the *mitsvot* of the Torah. [33]

V

R. Moshe Feinstein addresses the issue of the burial of non–halakhic converts in two responsa. In *Iggerot Moshe, Yoreh De'ah*, vol. 1, no. 160, after noting that a Conservative rabbi's conversion is halakhically ineffectual,[34] Rabbi Feinstein nonetheless does not feel that the burial in a Jewish cemetery of such converts is so overwhelmingly significant an issue as to warrant a potentially divisive fight to oppose it. Rather, opines Rabbi Feinstein, it suffices simply to alert the religiously observant Jews ("*shomerei Torah*") to the situation of these burials, so that they be advised not to bury their own dead next to the graves of these non–halakhic converts, and preferably that they retain a separation of eight *amot*. However, regarding non–religious Jews who wish to be buried in that cemetery, Rabbi Feinstein advises the questioner just to register his protest ("*rak limhot*") about the burial of these non–halakhic converts; after that, he not be concerned anymore:[35]

> Therefore your obligation is only to warn the *shomerei Torah* Jews [about the situation], so that they should command not to be buried near [non–halakhic converts like these. And it is advisable to be stringent (*ve–tov le–hahmir*) to separate (their graves) from those (graves of non–halakhic converts by at least) eight cubits. . . .[36] And regarding those Jews who are not *shomerei Torah* and who are indifferent [to the situation], you need only to

75

register your protest (about the burial of these non–halakhic converts) . . . but you are not obligated to create a controversy over this issue for the sake of the transgressors. And for the *shomerei Torah* Jews, it is sufficient that you warn them to (bury their dead) eight cubits away (from these non–halakhic converts).

It is significant to compare R. Feinstein's conclusions in the case of the burial of a non–Jewish spouse, referred to above, to his conclusions in this case here. Whereas in the former case he requires a fence of ten *tefahim* in addition to a separation of eight *amot*, no fence is necessary in the present case and the distance of eight *amot* is presented merely as a stringency–*tov le–hahmir*. In the former case, furthermore, R. Feinstein makes it clear that this requirement of separation is directed even for the burial of non–religious Jews; whereas his response in this case is clearly directed as being meant only for the burial of "*shomerei Torah*." Interestingly, in the first case R. Feinstein makes reference to the non–Jewish spouse's lack of *kedushat Yisra'el*, but no such mention is made in the case of the non–halakhic convert; the issue is presented solely in terms of "*ein koverin rasha etsel tsaddik*." [37] In general, the whole tone of R. Feinstein's response to the burial of non–halakhic converts appears to be more subdued than his response to the burial of non–Jewish marriage partners, though it is obvious that each has not acquired the strict halakhic status of being a Jew.

In a second responsum, *Iggerot Moshe, Yoreh De'ah*, vol. 2, no. 149, Rabbi Feinstein addresses the issue of the burial of a would be convert who was circumcised but did not undergo *tevillah* in the *mikveh*. The exact details of the case are not related, but one may surmise that the case deals with the child of a Jewish father and a non–Jewish mother who had a *berit milah* but never "completed" the process of *gerut* with *tevillah*.[38] In this case once again, it is clear that the deceased is not halakhically considered Jewish, as R. Feinstein himself points out:

Without *tevillah* even though he has already been circumcised, he is not (considered) a convert (to Judaism), and therefore he ought not be buried in a Jewish cemetery.

However, in the case referred to, the family has insisted on burying this "incomplete" convert in a Jewish cemetery. As such R. Feinstein, echoing what he wrote in his previous responsum, does not feel that the issue is so significant that the questioner need take a stand and actively fight against it:

However I do not see any obligation for the [local Orthodox] rabbis to contend with this [case]. . . . It suffices that they just protest that this deceased not be buried immediately next to the bodies that have already been interred in this cemetery, but [that there be] a separation of [at least] four cubits or (if this is impossible) that a fence be erected around those bodies that have already been interred.

Once again, in comparison with his earlier response about the Jewish burial of non–Jewish marriage partners, the tone here is more subdued. R. Feinstein instructs the questioner merely to protest, to ensure that the Jewish dead already interred in the cemetery remain at least four *amot* away from the grave of this "incomplete" convert. While R. Feinstein does admit that a distance of eight *amot* would be preferable,[39] he feels that a separation of four *amot* is sufficient. Alternatively, a fence may be erected in place of the four cubit separation. And R. Feinstein injects a new reason for his leniency:

> Also it is possible that a non–Jew who does not worship idols, like this one, who has already undergone circumcision *le–gerut* is better than an apostate [in regards to distance of burial from other Jews]. [40]

From both responsa it appears that R. Feinstein is of the opinion that a non–halakhic convert or an incomplete convert[41] has more privileges of Jewish burial than a regular non–Jew. In fact, in both responsa R. Feinstein clearly makes the comparison to the case of Jewish apostates referred to by *Gilyon Maharsha, Yoreh De'ah* 362.[42]

Furthermore, R. Feinstein's approach to require that the non–halakhic" incomplete" convert's grave be separated specifically from the graves of religiously observant Jews (*shomerei Torah*) is very similar to his approach in another responsum about the separation between the graves of those who are *mehallelei Shabbat be–farhesya* and those who are true *shomerei Torah*:

> If [the deceased] is well known as a Sabbath desecrator. . .they will have to separate from his grave eight cubits from the grave of an upright [religious] person. . .and if it is impossible to separate [eight cubits] because the space is tight, they will have to erect a wall of ten *tefahim* between [the two graves]. [43]

The proviso of separation from the graves of religious Jews is in line with the idea that a *rasha* should not be buried next to a *tsaddik*. It is not then a specific disability applied to non–halakhic "incomplete" converts.

If so, one might argue that though a non–Jew is not allowed burial in a Jewish cemetery, or is only allowed burial where there is clear and obvious separation from every other Jewish grave (i.e., eight *amot* plus a fence), a non–halakhie convert or an "incomplete" convert has attained some character of Jewish identity and thus one need not vigorously protest his or her burial on a Jewish cemetery. The only proviso, according to R. Feinstein, is that his grave not be alongside the graves of *shomerei Torah* Jews. It appears then, that the non–halakhic convert and the "incomplete" convert–though they clearly cannot be labeled Jewish according to the halakhic considerations of their status– have perforce entered some form of identification with the Jewish community which enables them–more than any other non–Jew to qualify for some form of limited burial privileges in the Jewish cemetery.[44]

It should be noted, however, that R. Feinstein's approach to the burial of non–halakhic converts is not universally accepted. R. Jehiel Jacob Weinberg, for example, in discussing the burial of non–halakhic converts, quotes R. Feinstein's first responsum; however, he very clearly disagrees with the conciliatory tone. R. Weinberg, in no uncertain terms, instructs his questioner to strictly enforce that the interment of non–halakhic converts in the Jewish cemetery take place only in a special row, separated by eight *amot* from all other "*kivrei*

Yisra 'el kesherim." Though he is definitely aware of the controversy that this stand will engender, R. Weinberg feels that a more lenient approach cannot be condoned.[45] Yet, strict as his approach is when compared to R. Feinstein's, R. Weinberg too accepts the burial of non–halakhic converts in a Jewish cemetery, provided they are interred in a separate row, something never permitted for other non–Jews.

VI

Our premise, that Jewish burial requires a less rigid Jewish identity than a formal halakhic Jewish status, gains strength from a responsum written by Rabbi Jekutiel Judah Greenwald concerning a convert who died, where doubts arose as to the halakhic validity of her *gerut*. Specifically, the doubts revolved about the propriety of the *beit din* which consisted of an unknown "reverend" and two laymen. These doubts were strengthened by the fact that the convert's husband was a *kohen*, a clear violation of Jewish law. On the other hand, all her acquaintances considered her to be Jewish and were apparently even unaware that she had not been born Jewish and had been converted. Furthermore she raised her children in the traditions of Judaism.[46]

After discussing the merits of the case, R. Greenwald allows her to be buried in the Jewish cemetery with the proviso that she be buried four *amot* away from "*kivrei Yisra 'el kesherim*." [47] In the course of his discussion, he offers two important points to permit her burial in a Jewish cemetery, even assuming that halakhieally she is not Jewish:

> 1. Furthermore, even those who do not adhere to the laws of Judaism but [simply] have abandoned their gentile religion and have died, surely it is necessary for us to bury them in a Jewish cemetery; for they have no other religion, and no other cemetery [of another denomination] will attend to their burial, for they have abandoned the faith of their birth and according to their own assumption have accepted the Jewish faith.[48]
> 2. Also if we do not accept her for burial (in a Jewish cemetery), this will cause a desecration of the Name [*hillul ha–Shem*], for what will people say; after all she has abandoned her [gentile] faith [for the Jews], and [now] no one [Jewish] will look after her [burial].[49]

In his second point R. Greenwald refers to a real danger of *hillul ha–Shem* if we do not accept for burial a non–Jew who has identified with the Jewish religion. His first point is more contestable, as one might argue for burial in a non–denominational cemetery. Nevertheless, R. Greenwald concludes that while her halakhic status may not be Jewish, her identification with Judaism has given her the qualifications for Jewish burial privileges.

It would seem that these statements can be applied to many non–halakhic converts, even to those performed under Reform auspices. These converts are not "incomplete" in the sense that they were prevented from completing a halakhic conversion; their conversion did not include any semblance of *beit din, kahbalat ha–mitsvot. milah* and *tevlilah le–shem gerut*. Yet in many cases, the person who has undergone even Reform ritual clearly identifies with the

Jewish religion. True, his or her halakhic status remains non–Jewish, but the subjective identification is Jewish; and, as we have seen, for some *posekim* this would suffice for limited burial privileges. Note that this is different from the case of the non–Jewish spouse referred to above, who did not undergo any form of "conversion" whatsoever and who retained allegiance to her gentile religion; the identity there is clearly non–Jewish, even regarding the issue of burial.

Similarly, R. Greenwald, commenting on the cases of *Tseror ha–Kesef* and *Minhat Elazar* discussed earlier (where the conversion remained incomplete at the time of death), adds the following comment:

> [Regarding] a non–Jew who accepted Judaism and died before he immersed in a *mikveh* [*le–shem gerut*], [the same halakhah applies]: even if he died before undergoing *berit milah*, if it is known to all that he accepted verbally and in his heart the faith of Judaism (*kibbel 'emunat Yisra'el be–libbo u–vis-fatav*) and that he renounced his previous religion and abandoned it (*hikh 'hish emunato ad az*) . . . he is to be buried in a Jewish cemetery.[50]

Here once again, the requirement presented for Jewish burial is not a halakhic conversion that create the halakhic status of Jew; rather it is the would–be convert's clear Jewish identification: the renunciation of the previous gentile religion and the true acceptance of the Jewish faith. One might argue that it is possible to include many non–halakhic converts under this formulation, even Reform converts, for Reform converts as well are asked to repudiate their Christian beliefs (*hikh 'hish emunato ad az*) and to accept the faith of the Jewish people (*kibbel emunat Yisra'el*). Of course, not every Reform convert will meet the test of clearly identifying with the Jewish religion, especially when the "conversion" is effected after only a quick and shallow course of study; furthermore, the theological and religious deviations of Reform Judaism to which such a convert would subscribe may not always qualify as *emunat Yisra'el*.[51] Yet based on R. Greenwald's approach, it seems that in cases where the non–halakhic converts have really committed themselves to the concepts of *hikh 'hish emunato ad az* and *kibbel emunat Yisra'el*, they could be granted some privileges in a Jewish cemetery.

VII

Needless to say, we are dealing here with a public policy issue, one that cannot be settled by simply quoting previously published *pesak*. There are serious–sometimes conflicting–personal and communal concerns which must be addressed and balanced. But any valid conclusion on policy requires an awareness of how *posekim* have dealt with the burial rights of incomplete or non–halakhic converts. Nothing less than a full halakhic conversion will suffice to attain Jewish status. However, true identification with the Jewish community has been recognized as having an effect in certain halakhic areas, and it should figure into the final decision regarding burial.

NOTES

I. One of the most reliable methods of tracing the spread of Jewish settlers and organized Jewish communities across the United States has been by noting the date on the oldest tombstone in the Jewish cemetery in every town; see for example, Rufus Learsi, *The Jews in America: A History* (N. Y., World Publishing, 1954), pp. 27–28, 33, 67, 73, 74; see also *Encyclopedia Judaica* (1972), vol. 5, p. 276.

2. To delineate an area for Jewish burial simply by surrounding the graves with an empty space of eight (or four) *amot* is not sufficient; rather a formal *gader* or *mehitsah* is also required. See, for example, R. Josef Schwartz, *Hadrai Kodesh* (Oradea n.d.), no. 86, p. 67; J. Greenwald, *Kol Bo al Avelut* vol. I, p. 163, par. 3; see also *Hatam Sofer* quoted by Greewald, *Ibid.*, p. 165, par. 6.

3. That the entire cemetery, including as yet unused land, has sanctity is clear from *Shiltei ha–Gibborim*, *Sanhedrin* end of chap. 6; this is summarized by Greenwald, p. 170, par. 21. See also J. M. Tukachinsky, *Gesher ha–Hayyim* (Jerusalem 1960), vol. I, pp. 284–286. Regarding the exact nature of the *kedushah* and *issur* of the *beit ha–kevarot*, see Tukachinsky, vol. 2, pp. 58 ff.

Many communities have the custom of consecrating the walled boundaries of a new cemetery by encircling them (usually seven times) and reciting special psalms and prayers. See for example, Greenwald, p. 163, par. 4: Tukachinsky, vol. I, pp. 301–302. It would appear that the purpose of this custom is the formal setting aside (*haktsa 'ah*) of the entire cemetery as hallowed ground.

4. See also Malbim s. v. *ki*, q. v. *Midrash Rabhah Ruth. parashah* 2:25.

5. Rashi implies that this requirement to tend to the burial arrangements of non–Jews applies only if their bodies were discovered together with the bodies of Jews. However Ran (commentary on Rif *s. v. koverin*) disagrees and writes that we are to tend to the arrangements even if the discovered bodies consist of only non–Jews; *q. v.* Rashba *s.v. ha*.

6. Hiddushei Rabhenu Crescas Vidal (= traditional Ritva, now printed in *Hiddushei ha Ritva*. ed. Mossad HaRav Kook, Jerusalem 1981. vol. 2, p. 107, *s.v. ve–ha*) is most emphatic. Ran (*loc. cit.*) and Ritva MS. (cd. Mossad HaRav Kook. vol. 2, p. 103, *s.v. tanu rabbanan*) explain the reason as due to *ein koverin rasha etsell tsaddik* (*Sanhedrin* 47a, but *q. v. infra*). This view is quoted in *Tur Yoreh De'ah* 367.

7. *Bah*, at the end of *Tur Yoreh De'ah* 151. On the wider implications of the term *darkhei shalom*, see Walter Wurzburger, "Darkei Shalom." *Gesher*. vol. 6,1977–1978, pp. 80–86.

8. Rabbi D. Hoffmann, in a responsum addressed to R. Bernat Schück, first printed in *Dat ve–Din. Hit es Allam* (Temesvar 1904), pp. 9–10 (Heb.), also printed in *Melammed le–Ho'il*, vol. 2, no. 127. See further below.

9. For a mystical explanation of the exclusiveness of Jewish burial in a Jewish cemetery, see the letter of R. Eliezer Deutsch to R. Schück (*Dat ve–Din*, p. 12, Heb.).

10. Even though R. Hayyirn Eliezer ben Isaac Or Zaru'a (*Or Zaru'a*. *Hilkhot Avelut* no. 422)had prohibited attending to the *kevurah* of a person who is known as a *ba'al averot*, *Bah* (at the end of *Tur Yoreh De'ah* 362) noted that the Talmud's phraseology *ein koverin rasha etsel tsaddik* (*Sanhedrin* 47a, quoted in *Tur* 362) implies clearly that a *rasha* is to be buried in a Jewish cemetery, albeit not next to a *tsaddik*. *Bah*'s opinion appears to be accepted (see for example, J. Greenwald, *op. cit.*, vol. I, p. 193). Similarly Rashba (*Responsa ha–Rashha* vol. 1, no. 763) concludes that heretics, apostates, suicides, and "poreshim mi–darkhei hatsibbur" are definitely accorded burial in a Jewish cemetery; the phrase *ein mit 'askin imahem* refers solely to our omitting *keri'ah*, *hesped*, and the like from the funeral service.

The specific issue of the burial of a *mumar* is referred to by R. Solomon Eiger in *Gilyon Maharsha*, *Yoreh De'ah* 362, and also in his *Iggerot Soferim*, no. 53: "yarhiku. . . yoter mi–shemoneh amot mi–kever Yisra 'el kasher." See *infra* n. 36. R. Moses Sofer (*Responsa Hatam Sofer, Yoreh De'ah* no. 341) discusses the case of an apostate Jew who died in the King's army–because the body was circumcised, it was assumed to be Jewish with a cross around his neck and was buried in a Jewish cemetery. While concurring that was correct, *Hatam Sofer* adds:

שלא כדין עשו שקברוהו בקברי ישראל הכשרים ופגעו בכבוד הצדיקים ההמה. איברא אחר שכבר נקבר לא נ"ל למעוטי שכבי.

His student, R. Hayyim Sofer (*Mahaneh Hayyim*, Jerusalem 1971, *Yoreh De'ah*. voL. 3, no. 49), in dealing with a similar case, decides likewise that the local *hevra kaddisha* is obligated to bury the *mumar* in the Jewish cemetery, but cautions that he be buried "*min ha–tsad.*" See further, R. Hayyim Medini, *Sedei Hemed, Asefat Dinim, s. v. avelut,* nos. 127–128; R. Eliezer Waldenberg, *Tsits Eliezer,* vol. 10, no. 41, part 2, pp. 215–219; Greenwald, vol. i, pp. 191–195. See *infra.* no. 44.

11. *Sefer Hayyim ba–Yad* on *Yoreh De'ah* (Jerusalem, reprint 1978). no. 99.

12. *Kol Bo,* vol. I, p. 194; similarly R. Gedalia Felder, *Nahalat Tsevi,* vol. 1, Toronto 1959, p. 139.

13. It is generally accepted that the offspring of a Jewish mother and a non–Jewish father is considered Jewish. However, it is interesting to note that R. Dov Berish Weidenfeld (*She'elot u– Teshuvot Dovev Meisharim,* Jerusalem 1951, no. 143, part 2), while requiring that such a child be buried in *kever Yisra'el* (and he instructs the he*vra kaddisha* to disinter the child's remains from a non–Jewish cemetery and reinter them in a Jewish cemetery), also stresses that the location of the grave be "*rahok mi–kivrel yeladim shel Yisra'elim.*" This is out of deference to the opinion of Rashi (*Kiddushin* 68b *s.v. leima* and *q.v. Maharsha Kiddushin* 75b *s. v. Tosabot: R. Yishma 'el*) that such a child does require conversion. R. Gedalia Felder delineates the distance of separation as eight *amot;* similarly R. Jehiel Jacob Weinberg, *Seridei Esh.* vol 3 (Jerusalem 1977), no. 100.

14. A few years ago this issue became a *cause celébre* in Israel in the case of a Christian woman, Teresa Angelovitch, who together with her husband had survived the Nazi concentration camps and had emigrated after the war to Israel. When she died in 1982, she was buried in the Jewish cemetery in Rishon le–Zion. Upon discovering that Mrs. Angelovitch was not Jewish and had never converted to Judaism, the town's Jewish burial society demanded that her body he exhumed and reburied in a segregated section of the cemetery. In March of 1984, it was found that her body had been surreptitiously disinterred from her grave and had been deposited in a corner of the Moslem cemetery in Ramle. The body was hastily reburied by police under orders of Israel's High Court of Justice (*Jerusalem Post,* March 6, 1984. pp. 1,2; March 7,1984, pp. 2,3; *N. Y. Times,* March 7,1984, sec. 1, p. 10).

15. This was compounded in certain areas of Europe by official government rules regulating the religious registration of the offspring of mixed marriages: sons followed the father's religion, daughters followed the mother's. This was the crux of the case discussed below by *Minhat Elazar;* see also *Dat ve–Din.* pp. 2, 26 (Heb.)

16. Temesvar, 1904. See also Greenwald, *op cit..* vol. I, p. 194; Felder, *op cit.,* p. 138.

17. *Dat ve–Din.* pp. 9–10 (Hebrew), later reprinted in *Melammed le–Ho 'il loc. cit.*

18. *Minhat Elazar* vol. 3 (reprint Bnei Brak 1968), no. 8; see above n. 15.

19. See for example, Greenwald, *loc. cit.*

20. That is to say: all other Jews who wish to be buried in accordance with halakhic requirements; sec following two notes.

21. *Iggerot Moshe. Yoreh De'ah.* vol. 3, no. 147. In another responsum regarding burial (*Iggerot Moshe. Yoreh De'ah,* vol. 2, no. 152), R. Feinstein equates eight cubits with five yards.

22. *Ibid.*

23. R. Moshe Steinberg, *Hukkat ha–Ger* (Rubin Mass, Jerusalem 1971), p.11, n. 1, quoting *She'elat Moshe, Yoreh De'ah,* no. 98.

24. For the sake of simplicity we have: used the term "non–halakhic convert" throughout this article, though, of course, we do not mean to offer legitimacy to such conversions. Perhaps a more accurate term would have been "quasi–convert" or "pseudo–convert."

25. R. Moshe Feinstein has explained that a "conversion" conducted by non–Orthodox rabbis has no halakhic validity because I) these rabbis do not require a proper and complete *kabbalat ha–mitsvot,* and 2) they are "*pesulin le–beit din,*" making them ineligible to perform conversions in the first place. Furthermore, in the case of female "converts," the *tevillah* docs not take place in the actual presence of their "*beit din.*" R. Feinstein clearly directs his statements even to Conservative conversions; see *Iggerot Moshe, Yoreh De'ah.* vol. i. no. 160.

26. See above n. 22.

27. That is, without the separation of a fence; cf. above n. 21.

28. *Tseror ha–Kesef* no. 18 (Salonika 1756; also quoted in *Ikkerei ha–Dat* on *Yoreh De'ah.* chap. 35, par. 40). It is interesting to note that nowhere in the discussion is there any mention of a separation between her grave and the other Jewish graves in the cemetery; cf. below.

29. *Zekan Aharon* (Constantinople 5494, reprint Jerusalem 1970), no. 19.

30. *Minhat Elazar loc. cit.* This case is discussed above.

31. The reason, R. Shapira explains, is because the would–be *ger* had undergone true self sacrifice

(*mesirat nefesh*) in his accepting the ideals of Judaism and by subjecting himself to the ritual of *berit milah*: to relegate his body now for burial in a non–Jewish cemetery would be both cruel and unfair. See further below n. 40.

32. *Ibid.* R. Felder's statement (p. 138), that according to *Minhat Elazar* "*yirhaku oto* arba *amot*," does not represent an accurate quotation.

33. Printed in *Sefer Milhamot Elohim, Being the Controversial Letters and the Casuistic Decisions. . . . By His Son,* H. Illoway (1914), pp. 149–154. The husband of the deceased contended that the rabbis in Holland who had performed the conversion had refused to provide a written certificate because of fear of the royal edict which strictly prohibited conversions. A similar case is discussed *infra*, n. 46.

34. *Supra*, n. 25.

35. R. Feinstein does require that at least a protest on behalf of the non–religious Jew be made, because though such Jews may be classified as *resha'im. yet le–khat 'hilah*, "*ein likvor . . . Yisra 'el rasha etsel akkum*." Furthermore, the possibility exists that they may have done *teshuvah* a moment before death, and consequently are not considered *resha'im*.

36. R. Feinstein bases his separation of eight cubits on *Gilyon Maharsha*, quoted above n. 10; see also below.

Similarly, in a case of bodies burnt beyond recognition, where it was impossible to determine Jewish identity with any degree of certainty, R. Aryeh Leibish Horowitz. *Harei Besamim, Mahadura Tinyana*, no. 222, permitted their burial in a Jewish cemetery, provided that their graves be separated from the other Jewish graves by eight *amot*.

37. *Sanhedrin* 47a. It is of course obvious from the first half of *Iggerot Moshe. Yoreh De'ah*, vol. I, no. 160–*supra* n. 25–that R. Feinstein definitely denies *kedushat Yisra'el* to a nonhalakhic convert.

38. It is a fact today that certain Orthodox *mohalim* in America will perform a *berit le–shem gerut* on the son of a Jewish father and a non–Jewish mother even in cases where it is clear that the parents do not intend to complete the *gerut* procedure and to have their child immersed in a *mikveh* (*le–shem gerut*) in the presence of a proper Orthodox *beit din*. While it is true that in these cases the *mohel* usually adds the notation "*ta'un tevillah*" on the certificate presented to the parents, if it is clear that the parents are concerned simply about the ritual of *berit milah* and have no intention of carrying out the "*ta'un tevillah*." one must wonder in terms of today's blurring of Jewish identities– at the wisdom of starting the process of *gerut* where it is obvious that its conclusion will not be reached.

39. Like *Gilyon Maharsha*, *supra* n. 36; see *infra*.

40. Cf. the *teshuvah* of R. Asher Lemil b. R. Abraham (originally printed in *Shomer Tsiyyon ha–Ne'eman*, vols. l54–15H, Altona 5613, now reprinted in *Sefer Yad Shelomoh*, Kollel Institute of Greater Detroit, N.Y, 1986, pp. 2–12) regarding the actual case of a would–be convert who had undergone *berit milah* and *kabbalat ha–mitsvot* but had not yet undergone *tevillah*, where he concluded that not only is he permitted to do *melakhah* on *Shabbat*, but אפי' מחויב ומוזהר על יום ולילה ...לא ישבותו וחייב לעשות מלאכה בשבת כל זמן שלא טבל לשם גירות The emphatic nature of his *pesak*–indeed the would–be *ger* was *forced* to write on Shabbat to underscore its validity–aroused the ire of other authorities and created a halakhic controversy (collected now in *Sefer Yad Shelomoh*, pp. 1–27). Of special interest to R. Feinstein's statement here is the opinion of R. Yitshak Ettlinger (*ibid.*, p. 14): דאף שעדיין לא נכנס לכלל ישראל גמור עד שטבל, מ"מ משעה שנכנס לברית מילה כבר נבדל מכלל בני נח. *Q.v. infra* n. 44; also Steinberg, *Hukkat ha–Ger*, pp. 105–106.

41. We have generally equated the status of "non–halakhic converts" and "incomplete converts." This equation has already been articulated by R. Weinberg, *loc. cit.*

42. See *supra* nn. 10,36,39.

43. *Iggerot Moshe. Yoreh De'ah.* vol. 2, no. 152.

44. It may be tentatively possible to formulate the Jewish identity of such non–halakhic" incomplete" converts by stating that they have attained *shem Yisra'el* without yet having acquired *kedushat Yisra'el* R. Aharon Lichtenstein ("Brother Daniel and the Jewish Fraternity," *Judaism.* Summer 1963, p. 268) has already concluded that a *mumar* retains his *shem Yisra'el*, though he loses his *kedushat Yisra'el*. See *supra* n. 10, that the burial of a *mumar* too, while permitted in a Jewish cemetery, is subject to certain restrictions. The statement by R. Yitshak Ettlinger, quoted

above in n. 40, would seem to support this formulation, at least for the incomplete convert (circumcised but not yet immersed). Similarly R. Moshe Steinberg, *op. cit.* p. 106, writes concerning an incomplete convert: מ"מ כבר נכנס בדת יהודית וחשוב גם קודם הטבילה בר הויה אבל בכל זאת אין בו קדושת ישראל.
Regarding semi–Jewish status, reference should also be made to an article by R. Zalman N. Goldberg in *Tehumin*, vol. 5, *Yihus Imahut...*, pp. 256–257. R. Goldberg, in discussing the case of a non–Jewish embryo transferred and implanted into the womb of a Jewish host mother, concludes that such a child, while requiring a full *gerut* to be considered Jewish, nonetheless retains (even after the *gerut*) a halakhic filial relationship to his Jewish host mother. The impact of this concept *mishpahat Yisra'el* without *shem Yisra'el*–on the discussion of our case requires further development and treatment. An English version of this article appeared in *Crossroads: Halacha and the Modern World* (Zomet, 1987), pp. 71–78.

45. *Seridei Esh, loc. cit.*
46. *Kol Bo*, vol. 2, pp. 68–70. A similar case is referred to above, n. 33.

Rabbi Saul Weiss of Brockton, Mass. has told me of a case he once discussed with R. Joseph B. Soloveitchik of Boston, regarding a woman married to a Jewish husband, who considered herself Jewish, kept certain basic Jewish holiday traditions, and was accepted as part of her Jewish community Upon her demise it was ascertained that she had not been born Jewish but had been converted fifty years earlier. No conversion papers were available, but it appeared probable that the conversion had been performed by a Reform rabbi. R. Soloveitchik's opinion was that as long as it was not known with certainty that she did *not* immerse in a *mikveh* at the time of the conversion (*le–shem gerut*), she could not be deprived of *kever Yisra'el*.

47. Cf. supra n. 45.
48. *Kol Bo*, vol. 2, p. 69; *q.v.* the statement of R. Judah b. R. Shalom in *Midrash Tanhuma, parashat Va–Yikra* par. 2.
49. *Kol Bo*, vol. 2, p. 70; cf. *Zekan Aharon, supra* n. 29.
50. *Kol Bo*, vol. I, p. 190, n. 21. 5 i.
51. For example, Reform's denial of Torah *min ha–shamayim* could be considered a serious disqualification from a true commitment to *Emunat Yisra'el* . On the other hand, not every Reform convert is so finely attuned to Reform theology as to have clearly enunciated such a theological denial.

CONVERSION AND THE ACCEPTANCE OF MITSVOT

Michael J. Broyde and Shmuel Kadosh

Review Essay

INTRODUCTION

Authors Avi Sagi and Zvi Zohar in *Transforming Identity: The Ritual Transition from Gentile to Jews–Structure and Meaning* undertake–in a time when many only ponder the minutiae–to examine one of the most complex problems confronting Orthodoxy: conversion to Judaism in modern times. The combination of massive Russian aliyah to Israel (including many who are not Jewish as a matter of halakha) and the significant intermarriage which has affected the Jewish community in America has made conversion to Judaism an important topic. However, after thoroughly reading this book, we conclude that the authors are mistaken in their central premise that conversion without a binding acceptance of *mitsvot* is possible as a matter of Jewish law, and that their conclusion is inconsistent with Talmudic, medieval, and modern Jewish law discourse.

This review will be divided into three sections. The first section examines the basic analytic insight of the book: that the two central Talmudic sources which discuss *giyyur* (conversion) are at odds with one another and that the halakha is uncertain which view is correct. The second section critiques specific but critically important source readings that the authors undertake, and the third argues that their basic framework for pondering acceptance of commandments is mistaken. The conclusion and postscript examine paths not taken.

Throughout this article, we will make reference to a number of closely related–but distinct–concepts, and we would like to clarify our terminology at the outset. *Hoda'at ha–mitsvot* refers to the education or notification of the commandments to the potential convert. *Kabbalat ha–mitsvot* refers to the convert's acceptance of Jewish law as binding upon himself. *Asiyat* or *shemirat ha–mitsvot* refers to the convert's actual observance of the *mitsvot*.

(These three concepts are factually unrelated to each other. A person can observe *mitsvot* that they do not accept as binding, and a person can accept as binding *mitsvot* that they do not observe. A person can be informed of *mitsvot* without ever accepting that he has to keep them. At first glance, one who has not thought about conversion rigorously might wonder how a person can accept the commandments without being informed of them. The answer is analytically simple. One can accept that one must obey a law that one does not understand. Indeed, upon reflection one sees that the process of becoming, for example, an American citizen requires that one pledge obedience to American law, for without that oath one can not become a citizen. Yet, the courses that one needs to take and the knowledge that one needs to have to become a citizen is a much less significant matter, and certainly one can become an American citizen while being informed of much less than "all" of American law.[1])

I. IS THE "*YEVAMOT* PARADIGM" IN TENSION WITH THE "*DEMAI* PARADIGM"?

The basic intellectual predicate of Zohar and Sagi's book is that the two central Talmudic sources addressing conversion–one a Tosefta in Demai, the other a running Talmudic discussion in Tractate *Yevamot* are in profound tension. The Tosefta in *Demai* emphasizes the convert's substantive acceptance of commandments ("*kabbalat ha–mitsvot*). It states (Tosefta *Demai* 2:4–5):

> A convert who accepted upon himself all matters of Torah, excepting one thing, should not be accepted [by the *Bet din*]. R. Jose son of Judah says: this includes even a small matter enacted by the scribes.

Bavli *Yevamot* (46a–48a), on the other hand, emphasizes the procedural components of conversion. It recounts a number of debates about the requirements of circumcision and immersion, without making any mention of *kabbalat ha–mitsvot*.

Sagi and Zohar maintain that these two *sugyot* are in tension with each other. The major thrust of their book is that a *bet din* can accept for conversion a person who has undertaken no *kabbalat ha–mitsvot* at all so long as that person has agreed to fulfill the *Yevamot* procedural of circumcision and immersion (or immersion alone for a woman). The authors attempt to divide the *Rishonim*, codes, and *Ahronim* into two groups: those who accept the *Demai* paradigm and those who accept the *Yevamot* paradigm, and the authors argue that most authorities accept the *Yevamot* procedural paradigm. With this mechanism, they undertake to defend conversion to Judaism even when the convert has never accepted the *mitsvot*.

For example, they state:

> Careful analysis of the sources led us to the understanding that there exist two variant voices on this issue in halakhic literature from Tannatic time to the present. Each position considers *giyyur* under a different concept. According to one position, *giyyur* is a voluntaristic normative commitment by which one acquires membership in a society defined primarily by normative praxis. We refer to this view as the *Demai* paradigm– . . According to the alternate position, *giyyur* is a ritual process by which one acquires membership in a society defined primarily by kinship. We refer to this view as the *Yevamot* paradigm. . . As we shall see, both paradigms exist concurrently during the entire history of halakhic literature... (107)

Further on, the authors state:

> We analyzed the *Yevamot* paradigm of *giyyur*. According to this paradigm, *giyyur* is a ritual process focused upon the body of the proselyte. This process consists of no more than two components: circumcision and immersion. (136)

87

The *Yevamot* paradigm, they claim, is conversion without any *kabbalat ha–mitsvot*. They repeat this basic view many times in the book and it is the thrust of chapters 5–11. The authors themselves have elsewhere noted that this is the basic theme of the book.[2]

This insight–that the Talmudic sources are in profound tension and that the *Rishonim* divide along the lines of the competing *sugyot*–is an unprecedented analysis of the Jewish law of conversion and, in our opinion, incorrect. The classic sources do not support the very existence of such dispute. Eminent *Rishonim* who comfortably note in other places that *sugyot* in the Talmud are in tension, and found no difficulty in resolving such tension by picking one *sugya* over another, do not mention any dispute here. Thus, we find this fundamental distinction to be unsubstantiated and without halakhic support.

For example, let us examine the view that Zohar and Sagi consider to be the paradigm of this approach–Maimonides. Maimonides begins his discussion of conversion with what seems to be an unequivocal requirement for *kabbalat ha–mitsvot*. In *Hilkhot Issurei Biah* 13:4, he states:

> So too in every generation, when a gentile wishes to enter into the Covenant and seek shelter under the wings of the *Shekhinah*, and he accepts upon himself the yoke of Torah, he needs circumcision, immersion, and bringing a sacrifice...

Later in the chapter, Maimonides discusses the wives of Samson and Solomon who converted despite their improper motivation for conversion (namely, marriage) and lack of observance. Maimonides concludes that while such conversions should not be done *ab initio*, after the fact, they are accepted. He writes (*Hilkhot Issurei Biah* 13:17):

> A convert whose motives were not investigated or was not informed of the commandments but was circumcised and immersed in the presence of three laymen, is a proselyte. Even if it becomes known that he became a convert for some ulterior motive, he has exited from the Gentile collective, because he was circumcised and immersed.

Sagi and Zohar maintain that Maimonides adopts the *Yevamot* paradigm, and accepts conversion after the fact even without an acceptance of the *mitsvot*. They argue that halakha 4 (requiring *kabbalat ha–mitsvot*) represents the ideal conversion, while halakhot 14–17 (which they argue do not require a *kabbalat ha–mitsvot*) list the minimal requirements for conversion (166–170). Such a distinction is unfounded in the text, nor is it adopted by subsequent commentators.[3] Sagi and Zohar maintain that halakha 17 waives the requirement for *kabbalat ha–mitsvot*, at least after the fact. However, we are persuaded that a careful reading of halakha 17 indicates that Maimonides was only willing to waive the requirement of notifying the convert of the commandments (*hoda 'at ha–mitsvot*); nowhere does Maimonides actually waive the requirement for *kabbalat ha–mitsvot* articulated in halakha 4. By steadfastly refusing to draw an obvious linguistic and substantive distinction between *hoda'at ha–mitsvot* (informing of the commandments) and *kabbalat ha–mitsvot* (acceptance of the commandments), Zohar and Sagi misunderstand the Maimonidean position.[4]

Michael J. Broyde and Shmuel Kadosh

In addition, many other difficulties are created within the view of Maimonides if we assume that *kabbalat ha–mitsvot* is not required for conversion even after the fact, not the least of which is why Maimonides would insist that *kabbalat ha–mitsvot* is needed by slaves (*Issurei Biah* 12:1 1) but not converts.

The authors compound this mistake with an out of context quotation of the *Bah* (Sagi and Zohar, at 170; *Bah*, YD 268, s.v. *ve–kol inyanav*). They quote the *Bah* as stating the following:

> Maimonides... requires three only for immersion . . . for it is then that he becomes a proselyte . . . Our master Maimonides wrote that the *giyyur* is valid even if it was totally lacking in intent to accept the commandments. *(ellipses in original)*

In fact, when learned in its entirety, a very different picture of the Bah emerges. In this section, the *Bah* discusses the dispute between the *Ba'alei ha–Tosafot* and Rambam about the central judicial ritual of conversion. *Tosafot* posit that the central judicial ritual in conversion is *kabbalat ha–mitsvot* which must take place in front of a *bet din*, whereas circumcision and immersion need not take place before a rabbinical court. Rambam, on the other hand, posits that immersion in a *mikveh* (and perhaps circumcision for a man) is the central judicial framework for conversion and it is these rituals which must take place in front of a *bet din*. According to this view, *kabbalat ha–mitsvot* is merely a prerequisite for a valid conversion that is then consummated before a rabbinical court. The *Bah* summarizes this dispute as follows:

> According to Rif, Rambam, and *Smag* . . . immersion requires three (and so it is according to the first answer of Maharam). This is unlike the approach of *Tosafot* and the second answer of Maharam. When there were three [judges] for the immersion, Maimonides wrote that it is valid, despite not having been done for the sake of *kabbalat ha–mitsvot* at all. The *Tosafot* and Rosh argue that the absence of *kabbalat ha–mitsvot* certainly invalidates conversion. They state that we should not marry him until he accepts the *mitsvot* in front of three.[5]

When read in its totality, it is fairly clear that the *Bah* is merely claiming that at the time of immersion, the *immersion* need not be for the sake of *kabbalat ha–mitsvot*. The *Bah* certainly does not say that a conversion can take place in the total absence of *kabbalat ha–mitsvot* and still be valid. Rather, the *Bah* requires acceptance of the *mitsvot* at some point, just not immersion for that purpose.

Furthermore elsewhere the *Bah* himself makes clear that *kabbalat ha–mitsvot* required for conversion. In the previous chapter (*Tur*, YD 267), which deals with acquiring slaves, *Bah* repeatedly compares and contrasts a slave, who does not require *kabbalat ha–mitsvot* in his view, with a convert, who does. Nowhere does the *Bah* indicate that a significant contingent of the prominent *Rishonim* (namely, Rambam, Rif, and *Smag*) disagree with this position and do not require *kabbalat ha–mitsvot* for converts, either.[6]

The only authority that Sagi and Zohar cite who unambiguously accepts the view that Rambam does not require *kabbalat ha–mitsvot* is the *Bet Meir* (Responsum 12). We are inclined to think that this citation is of little value because the *Bet Meir* makes this claim about the view of Rambam while explaining why normative halakha rejects this view, as he does himself. While it seems obvious to us, it may be worth stating that the intellectual value to normative Jewish law of the view of Maimonides as understood and rejected by the *Bet Meir* is close to none. One cannot, so to speak, rely on the *Bet Meir's* understanding of the Rambam, given that *Bet Meir* rejects Rambam's view.

More generally, while we acknowledge that there is a small group of *Ahronim* who ponder the possibility that Rambam does rule that a conversion done without *kabbalat ha-mitsvot* is valid after the fact,[7] we are hard pressed to find a single such authority who both states that this is the view of Maimonides and rules that the halakha is like the view of Maimonides, a central measure of whether anyone actually rules that way. Even more generally, *Ahronim*, when they encounter a *Rishon* that is difficult to categorize, will at times interpret that *Rishon* as a straw man so as to make clear that such an opinion is not normative such that it can be completely discounted. That seems to be what *Bet Meir* (and others) are doing here.

Sagi and Zohar (171) make a similar mistake in their analysis of Ritva. They begin by contrasting Ritva's words in *Ketubot* (11a, s.v. *Amar Rav Nachman, Amar Rav Huna*), that notification of the commandments is not essential, with Ritva in *Yevamot* (46b, s.v. *u–shema minei, ein matbilin ger ba–layla*), that a court is necessary for the immersion, even *post facto*. From this, they derive that "For Ritva, then, circumcision and immersion, and not acceptance of the commandments arc the necessary components of *giyyur*" (172). Once again, it seems that Sagi and Zohar mistake notification of the commandments for acceptance. In fact, as Sagi and Zohar note in a footnote (176, n. 1), Ritva himself clearly does require *kabbalat ha-mitsvot*. Instead of adopting the simpler explanation (namely, that Ritva waived a requirement for notification, and not acceptance), they contend that "in maturity he became convinced of the superiority" of the procedural paradigm. In fact, Ritva is merely accepting the correctness of both paradigms, so to speak–each in a different place in the Talmud. Ritva fits simply into the model in which notification of the commandments– but not their acceptance by the convert–is not needed for a valid conversion, just like Maimonides.

Sagi and Zohar (170–171) further compound their misreading of Rambam by seeking to relate him to the view of *Tosafot* that the conversion of a minor child can be performed without acceptance of *mitsvot*. They argue that this demonstrates that *kabbalat ha-mitsvot* is not needed for an adult, since it is not needed for a child. This logic is contrary to a basic axiom of Talmudic logic that we do not analogize from circumstances where performance is impossible to circumstances where performance is possible. Thus, the Talmud rejects the argument that circumcision is unnecessary for male conversion because women are not circumcised. Similarly, *Tosafot* and Rosh accept that a man without a penis does not require circumcision for his conversion to be valid, because that would be impossible (*Tur and Bet Yosef YD* 268). In a similar vein, *Tosafot* aver that a child, lacking the capacity to accept anything, may convert without *kabbalat ha-mitsvot*(*Tur, Bet Yosef and Bah, YD* 268). But just as the first view of *Tosafot* (that a man without a sexual organ need not be circumcised) is not proof to the proposition that circumcision is not generally needed for conversion, so too the latter position (that a child need not have *kabbalat ha–mitsvot* to convert) in no way supports a similar argument with regard to *kabbalat ha-mitsvot* for adults.

Indeed, Sagi and Zohar's central proposition–that the existence of a *Rishon* discussing the procedures of conversion while not simultaneously addressing its substance is an indication that there is a tension between the two approaches, and that the *Rishon* therefore accepts that the procedural component alone is enough–is unsupported by the Talmudic literature or the medieval codes.

Two obvious proofs can be put forward to further sharpen this observation. The *Shulhan Arukh* effortlessly sews together these two Talmudic paradigms in one seamless chapter of his code, and in his pre–code analysis of this topic (*Bet Yosef YD* 268) it is never noted that the Talmudic sources, *Rishonim*, or the earlier medieval codes are in any tension on this issue. This certainly is not because such is not the style of the *Bet Yosef*–he was quite comfortable noting *sugyot* in tension and *Rishonim* disagreeing. That such a central dispute would elude the *Bet Yosef* is nearly impossible to believe.

Indeed *Tur* and *Bet Yosef* are acutely aware of a central disagreement that is in fact present between Rambam and *Tosafot*, but it is one which is a shadow of the dispute which Sagi and Zohar imagine. The actual dispute relates only to which stages in the conversion ritual require a court's presence. According to *Tosafot*, the court must be present for *kabbalat ha–mitsvot*, while according to the Rambam, it must be present for circumcision and immersion. Of course, just as *Tosafot* acknowledge that a valid conversion requires all three components, and they merely discuss which parts must take place in front of the judges, Rambam also accepts that all three actions must take place, but merely disagrees about which one (s) require(s) the presence of a rabbinical court.[8]

Like the *Shulhan Arukh* after him, the *Tur* not only rules that *kabbalat ha–mitsvot* is needed, he is completely unaware of a view that *kabbalat ha–mitsvot* is not needed. Rather, he harmonizes the *Demai sugya* with the *Yevamot sugya* and sees only a dispute about what needs to be done before a rabbinical court. All the views, according to the *Tur*, require circumcision, immersion, and acceptance of *mitsvot*. The same should be said for the view of R. Caro in both the *Shulhan Arukh* and the *Bet Yosef*.

In general, unified theories of halakha are superior to fractured theories. The attempt by Sagi and Zohar to paint the rules of conversion as a grand dispute between two Talmudic *sugyot* and two camps among the *Rishonim* does not withstand rigorous textual analysis. Rather, what we have is merely two sides of the same conversion coin, approached from different directions and with different nuances by the Talmud, *Rishonim*, and *Ahronim*.

Sagi and Zohar attempt to create a dispute between *sugyot* and *Rishonim* concerning whether *kabbalat ha–mitsvot* is needed or not, but in fact no such dispute exists. Rather, a much less important dispute is present–does a *bet din* need to be present for all three needed steps in the conversion process, or just one of them? Proof of this is simply that later *Rishonim* and codifiers do not mention this dispute at all. Neither Rosh nor Rashba among the later *Rishonim*, nor the *Tur* and *Shulhan Arukh* among the early codifiers, nor even *Arukh ha-Shulhan* and the many subsequent *Ahronim* who discuss the precise parameters of *kabbalat ha-mitsvot* note the scope and magnitude of this alleged Talmudic dispute. The reason is because such a dispute simply does not exist. Indeed, all of these sources and many more clearly state that *kabbalat ha-mitsvot* is needed for conversion. No classical sources state directly that *kabbalat ha-mitsvot* is not needed in contrast to the plethora of classic sources that repeat the simple formulation of the *Shulhan Arukh* (*YD* 268:3) that "*kabbalat ha-mitsvot* is a necessary requirement [for conversion] and must be done during the day and in front of three judges."

The reason no classical sources assert Sagi and Zohar's tension is that, in fact, R. Joshua's argument in *Yevamot* (46b) demonstrates the exact opposite—the basic unity of the *sugyot*. R. Joshua logically infers that immersion is a requirement of conversion, "for, otherwise, with what did they [the women] enter under the wings of the *Shekhinah*?" Implicit in R. Joshua's statement is that "entering under the wing of the *Shekhinah*" is a part of, and possibly defines, the *geirut* process.[9] Without entering into the debate as to the precise meaning of the phrase, it suffices to note that such a phrase carries with it theological connotations. The phrase "entering under the wings of the *Shekhinah*" conveys the sense that conversion involves a commitment to religious praxis (similar to "the yoke of heaven") and is not merely a ritual process. Contrary to the assertions of Sagi and Zohar, *Yevamot* represents not merely a "ritual process focused upon the body of the proselyte" but also an awareness of the binding religious obligation that is part of conversion.[10]

II. SPECIFIC TEXTUAL MISREADS BY ZOHAR AND SAGI

Aside from the issue discussed in Section 1, this book suffers from a tendency to over-read, under-read, and occasionally even misread sources. Occasional ambiguity is intrinsic to the writing of law, and a secondary writer examining the literature should not parse ambiguities as anything other than ambiguous. Yet, consistently throughout this work, Sagi and Zohar over-read and under-read when it is not textually called for. Furthermore, they seem to do so with a bias in favor of diminishing the requirement of *kabbalat ha-mitsvot*.

One example of this can be found in Chapters 8 and 9 of this book. The authors cite a number of *Geonim* and *Rishonim* (including Rif) who simply state that a convert must be "*mekabbel*" ("accept"). They deduce from here that these authorities reject a requirement for *kabbalat ha-mitsvot*, simply because the term "*kabbalat ha-mitsvot*" is not used. In fact, Rif's silence can at most he construed as ambiguous with regards to *kabbalat ha-mitsvot*. He could have used the term "*mekabbel*" as shorthand for "*kabbalat ha-mitsvot*," or he could have been referring to something else entirely. It is a significant over-reading of Rif to argue that his silence proves that he rejects a requirement of *kabbalat ha–mitsvot*. Indeed, the *Shiltei Giborim* (commenting on this Rif) reads Rif to be saying the exact opposite of what Sagi and Zohar claim; he insists that Rif does not require a *bet din*, but does require *kabbalat ha–mitsvot*.

This tendency to over–read can also be found in the authors' presentation of the *Shulhan Arukh's* view (200–217). In YD 268:3, R. Caro rules, "The acceptance of the commandments invalidates [the conversion] unless performed in the daytime and before three [judges]." Nine paragraphs later (YD 268:12), he writes:

> When a person comes forth with the intention of becoming a proselyte, they [the judges] should investigate: perchance he comes to enter the religion in order to gain money, or to qualify for a position of authority, or out of fear.. If they did not investigate his motivation, or did not inform him of the commandments and the punishment for transgressing them, but he was circumcised and immersed in the presence of three laymen, he is a proselyte. Even if it is known that he became a proselyte for some ulterior motive, he has exited from the heathen collective because he was circumcised and immersed.

Sagi and Zohar see tension between these two sections; paragraph 3, which requires *kabbalat ha–mitsvot*, accords with the *sugya* in *Demai*, while paragraph 12, which they argue does not require *kabbalat ha–mitsvot*, is in line with *Yevamot* (201). They proceed to delineate three ways of resolving this "internal contradiction" in the *Shulhan Arukh*. Once again, Sagi and Zohar have failed to make the critical distinction between acceptance and notification of the commandments. The only requirement the *Shulhan Arukh* waives in paragraph 12 is the notification of the commandments–never the acceptance. Thus there is no tension in need of resolution.

A more troubling example of this under–reading can be found in the authors' discussion of R. Moshe Feinstein's view of conversion. R. Feinstein has no less than twelve *teshuvot* on the role of *kabbalat ha–mitsvot* in conversion.[11] In them, he articulates a highly complex and nuanced view of conversion, but it is one in which acceptance of the commandments is the central ritual. He unambiguously and definitively requires a *kabbalat ha–mitsvot*. For example, he writes in *Iggerot Moshe*, YD 1:157 that a convert who did not accept the *mitsvot* "is clearly not a convert, even after the fact." Yet, Sagi and Zohar relegate R. Feinstein's view to one peculiar quote of an anomalous *teshuva* that surely does not represent the full view of R. Feinstein in any way. The authors then summarize R. Feinstein's view as saying, "Rabbi Feinstein assumes that there can be no *giyyur* without circumcision and immersion. This provides the ground enabling him to decide in favor of the first option: even if the acceptance of commandments is not full, the *giyyur* can be affected by the other two elements." (113) They do so in order to argue that R. Feinstein would accept as valid a conversion done without full acceptance of *mitsvot*, and that R. Feinstein ultimately accepts their version of the *Yevamot* paradigm.[12] This position is stunningly wrong to anyone familiar with the details of R. Feinstein's *teshuvot* dealing with conversion. This remarkably mistaken analysis of a halakhic authority who, more than any *posek* in the last seventy–five years, closely analyzed the rules of conversion and developed them into a coherent theoretical framework, is an inexplicable lacuna in a book addressing modern conversion in Jewish law.

Another particularly egregious example of Sagi and Zohar's misreading can be found in their analysis of the *Bet Meir* (211–215). Sagi and Zohar present R. Posner (the author of the *Bet Meir*) as a major *posek* of modern times who reads the Talmud and codes as they do, and does not require *kabbalat ha–mitsvot*. They title their discussion of R. Posner's position "Rabbi Meir Posner: re–validation of the *Yevamot* paradigm." They quote Posner as saying that "the crux of accepting the commandments is in that she commits herself in the presence of the court to immerse for the purpose of *giyyur*." In a footnote (217, n. 22) at the end of the chapter, they note that Posner offers an alternate explanation that does require *kabbalat ha–mitsvot*, but maintain that he had a "clear preference" for the *Yevamot* paradigm. Sagi and Zohar's analysis of this *teshuva* is wrong and misleading. It is true that the *Bet Meir* suggests that *kabbalat ha–mitsvot* is unnecessary–as a *hava amina*, a hypothetical and ultimately rejected possibility! However, this tentative hypothesis is decisively rejected at the end of the same responsa wherein R. Posner unequivocally states that *kabbalat ha–mitsvot* is necessary (*Respona Bet Meir*, 72–73). Indeed, this ruling is the basis of the ultimate *pesak* of the responsum–namely, that the conversion being discussed (which lacked a *kabbalat ha–mitsvot* in front of a *bet din*) is invalid. Sagi and Zohar have disingenuously taken a theoretical hypothesis of the *Bet Meir* and presented it as normative halakha, while relegating the actual conclusion to a footnote.

So too, we do not agree with the authors' reading of Responsum 92 of Ra' anah R. Eliyahu B. Hayyim (197–198). Sagi and Zohar claim that Ra'anah is the "first halakhist who consciously weighs alternative modes of understanding *kabbalat ha–mitsvot*." We do not see such a concept in this *teshuva*. In fact, Ra'anah states clearly that *kabbalat ha–mitsvot* is needed and a conversion is void without it. He does speculate that it is possible that *kabbalat ha–mitsvot* can take place in the *mikveh* (and it is worth noting that contemporary practice directs *dayanim* to have the convert repeat *kabbalat ha–mitsvot* in the *mikveh* again), but he never state–as Zohar and Sagi claim he does–that "immersion for the purpose of *giyyur* constitutes, *ipso facto*, the required acceptance." Indeed, Ra'anah makes it completely clear that although *kabbalat ha–mitsvot* can take place before or after immersion, acceptance of the *mitsvot* is needed in every case. So too, the statement of Sagi and Zohar, that "acceptance of commandments is a commitment made by the proselyte in the presence of the court to immerse for the sake of *giyyur*" is a woefully incomplete sentence. Ra'anah actually states that the reason immersion does not require a *bet din*–and only *kabbalat ha–mitsvot* does–is because (according to one *hava amina* that he puts forward) the *kabbalat ha–mitsvot* includes the intention that immersion will take place, but not that it is limited to merely immersing.

Another example can be found in Sagi and Zohar's analysis (209) of R. Yechezkel Landau, who writes in his *Dagul Merevavah* commentary to *Shulhan*

Arukh (YD 268:3) that there is a distinction between the conversion of a minor, where a *bet din* is required for circumcision and immersion, and the conversion of an adult, where such is not required. Sagi and Zohar write:

> In this text, Rabbi Landau postulates two very different processes of *giyyur*. For adults, the crux of *giyyur* is cognitive–acceptance of commandments–while circumcision and immersion are merely formal terminations of the process. For minors, the crux of *giyyur* is physical immersion–and there is no cognitive clement at all. Adult *giyyur* follows the *Demai* paradigm, while minors become full proselytes under the *Yevamot* paradigm. On this view, Torah itself follows two divergent paradigms, one for adults and one for minors. Rabbi Landau therefore presents Torah as advocating two incompatible views of the meaning of *giyyur*. In fact, this weakness characterizes the position of any scholar who holds the *Demai* paradigm but acknowledges that the *giyyur* of a minor is valid under Torah law. (*notes omitted*).

Upon close analysis of the words of the *Dagul Merevavah*, however, one does not, as these authors present, see a tension between the supposed *Demai* and *Yevamot* paradigms, but a standard analytic distinction. All that R. Landau means to say is that the central ritual of conversion is acceptance of *mitsvot* and that both the *Demai sugya* and the *Yevamot sugya* are correct whenever both can apply–but when one *sugya* cannot apply, then of course it does not. For a child who cannot willfully accept the *mitsvot*, the court must instead witness some other act of conversion.[13]

Sagi and Zohar similarly misread Ramban. In their view, the "acceptance" that Nahmanides requires of the convert is not an acceptance of the yoke of commandments, but an acceptance to go through with the rituals of conversion, namely, to circumcise and immerse (187). In support of this contention, they quote Nahmanides (*Yevamot* 45b, s.v. *mi lo tavla*):.. "If he was notified about some of the rewards and punishments for the commandments and accepted upon himself in court to be circumcised and immerse.. ." This quote is supposed to support their contention that "acceptance" refers only to immersion. However, if one reads beyond this small excerpt of Ramban, it is clear that this is not what Nahmanides meant. Further along in that paragraph, Nahmanides writes, "Even a male convert that accepts prior to circumcision should accept again at the time of immersion." Clearly, this acceptance at the time of immersion is not an "acceptance to immerse" as Sagi and Zohar claim. The convert is in the middle of immersing–he would scarcely need to verbally commit to perform an act that he is in the middle of performing! Sagi and Zohar compound this erroneous misread of Ramban when they claim (223–224) that this view (that acceptance means a commitment to immerse) is held by all the major halakhic authorities, including *Tosafot*, the *Tur* and *Shulhan Arukh*. The only authority they cite for this sweeping assertion is the *hava amina* of the *Bet Meir* which, of course, was subsequently rejected by the *Bet Meir* himself (as we explained above).

In this section, we have sampled a number of instances where it seems that Sagi and Zohar have misrepresented the various prooftexts they present throughout the book. In truth, the consistent misreading of sources undermines the basic value of the work itself. While every word they quote is in its place, the editing of quotes is done in a way that substantially misrepresents the meaning of the rabbinic works they quote.

III. WHAT IS THE DISPUTE ABOUT
ACCEPTANCE OF COMMANDMENTS?

Taking all of the above into account, there is no denying that there is indeed a dispute amongst *Rishonim* and *Ahronim* concerning the nature of *kabbalat ha–mitsvot*. However, as we described above, the dispute is not the profound dispute Sagi and Zohar put forward as to whether *kabbalat ha–mitsvot* is actually necessary at all. Until the writings of R. Uzziel, there is not a single halakhic authority who states that *kabbalat ha–mitsvot* is not necessary.' [14] In place of this deep schism that Sagi and Zohar suggest, there is instead a complex, nuanced dispute among *Rishonim* and *Ahronim* concerning the relationship between the acceptance of commandments required of converts and their subsequent lack of observance of the commandments.

That such a dispute should exist seems reasonable. As R. Herzog notes (*Pesakim u–Khetavim*, YD 89, 92, as well as R. Abraham *Dov Ber Kahana, Devar Avraham*, vol. 3, no. 28.), in times of old, fidelity to Jewish law was culturally normative, and the notion that one could become Jewish in a society in which all observed Jewish law but the convert would not observe was certainly far-fetched. In modern times, fidelity to Jewish law is not the popular *sine qua non* of Jewish identity. Thus the question of whether acceptance of *mitsvot* needs to be understood as identical with observance is asked. A survey of the twentieth century *Ahronim* reveals the full spectrum of possible answers to this question.

The first view is that of R. Moshe Feinstein (*Iggerot Moshe*, YD 1:157 and 1:160), who argues that *kabbalat ha–mitsvot* has to be understood as requiring a genuine desire for full and complete observance. Thus a convert cannot be accepted unless his acceptance is complete, and anything short of that is indicative of fraudulent or bogus acceptance. Of course, this view recognizes that converts, no different from anyone else, and sometimes out of ignorance and sometimes from temptation. But, R. Feinstein asserts, a conversion cannot be valid unless the convert sincerely intends to obey Jewish law as the convert understands it, in all its facets at the time of conversion, and that is measured generally by looking at practical levels of observance at the time of conversion.

The second view is that of the *Hazon Ish* (*YD*, 119:2), who understands *kabbalat ha–mitsvot* not in its practical sense as R. Feinstein does, but rather in its theological sense. A convert must accept, the *Hazon Ish* avers, the chosen uniqueness of the Jewish people as it relates to our role in this world. In this view, conduct consistent with Jewish law is but an external measure of an internal religious orientation. The reverse is also true–refusal to obey the *mitsvot* is an indication of a lack of acceptance of the nature of the Jewish people as a whole.

The third view is that of R. Hayyim Ozer Grodzinski (*Responsa Ahiezer* 3:26), as well as many others, who aver that *kabbalat ha–mitsvot* need not be accompanied by full and complete observance, but instead needs to be accompanied by observance of significant cultural features of Orthodox Jewish life such as Shabbat, *kashrut*, and family purity (*taharat ha–mishpaha*). It seems R. Grodzinski could well imagine converting a person to Judaism whose intellectual fidelity to Jewish law is complete but whose observance is incomplete. For example, a *bet din* may accept a potential convert who knows that gossip is a sin but confesses to the rabbinical court at the time of their conversion that they are one hundred percent certain that they will inevitably and regularly gossip at *kiddush* following Shabbat services even though they know such conduct to be wrong.

Another notable view among the *Abronim* is that of B.. David Zvi Hoffman (*Responsa Melamed le–Ho'il EH* 3:8), allowed a woman to be converted even though he knew she intended to marry a man who is a Kohen (with whom she was already living). R. Hoffman holds, as does R. Shmelkes (*Responsa Bet Yitshak*, YD 2:100), that there are situations in which a convert may be accepted even though he or she will not keep a particular matter (such as the prohibition against a Kohen marrying a convert), so long as their acceptance of Jewish law is generally complete.[15]

It is even possible to point to a group of *Ahronim* who could be understood as saying that even when we know that *shemirat ha–mitsvot* will generally be lacking, *kabbalat ha–mitsvot* is minimally acceptable so long as there is an acceptance by the convert of the obligation to observe *mitsvot* and the recognition that the non–observance of *mitsvot* is sinful. One could read such a view into the writings of R. Uzziel, R. Shlomo Goren, and others. In fact, some in this group might even be making a more complex claim, namely that a clear and direct articulated acceptance of commandments in front of the *bet din* is sufficient after the fact, even if the rabbinical court knows that this acceptance of commandments is insincere, since there is an articulated acceptance of *mitsvot*. That seems to be the view of the Gra commenting on *YD* 269:12.[16]

As with many matters of Jewish law, there is no firm resolution of this dispute, and individual halakhic authorities should function based on what they understand the normative halakha to be." However, the claim by Sagi and Zohar that there is a stream of thought in the Jewish tradition that allows for conversion without the acceptance of *mitsvot* at all for an adult who is mentally capable of accepting *mitsvot* would seem to be without foundation in the classic sources, and the sources they cite for support of their position in the Talmud, *Rishonim*, and early codes do not in fact support such a view.

CONCLUSION

Transforming Identity is a bold book that undertakes to examine from the perspective of halakha the most vexing problem of Orthodox Jewish life in Israel and one of the most challenging problems of Jewish life in America. It takes courage, wisdom, and an exquisite knowledge of rabbinics in all of its many facets to successfully write a persuasive analysis of Jewish law that addresses the topic of conversion. This book, while well-intentioned, ultimately fails in its reading of the rabbinic tradition and Jewish law. Its basic arguments–that the two Talmudic sources discussing conversion are in tension with each other, and that while some *Rishonim* accept one and require *kabbalat ha-mitsvot*, some accept the other source and do not require *kabbalat ha-mitsvot*–is without precedent and includes a glaring misunderstanding of the Jewish legal system.

POSTCRIPT

So what is the solution to the conversion conundrums in Israel and America? We confess that there are times when Jewish law simply cannot achieve the result desired by some people, and we must therefore struggle on with our lives, seeking to obey our Creator's will even as the results do not appeal to us. This is not unique to Jewish law, but is endemic to every legal system with timeless principles. Within Jewish law, this situation is not limited to issues related to conversion and anyone familiar with Jewish law sees such results on occasion. Of course, we should struggle to reach the best result possible in every case, but the struggle has to be grounded in a proper understanding of the classic sources, and solutions which are not grounded in the sources ought not to be followed. In each and every situation, there are those who declare that communities committed to Jewish law should throw in the towel and abandon the halakhic system as an act of kindness to suffering human beings. Yet all Jews who believe that Jewish law derives from God's will and revelation understand that it supersedes our wants and wishes. So, in such cases we struggle on, seeking to do that which halakha demands of us and acting with compassion to all.

Yet in the area of conversion, there is perhaps a possible solution to what ails us, and it is on much firmer ground in Jewish law than the solution proposed in the book being reviewed. There is a large number of Russians in Israel who are culturally and socially, but not halakhically Jewish. The writing of R. Moshe Feinstein have shown the way to a realistic solution[18] to this and many other conversion problems, particularly in Israel where Jewish identity is a more central concern. R. Moshe permits the regular conversion of minors into Judaism, so as to create, after the passage of many years, a society in which all those who think they arc Jewish, actually are. Unlike the conversion of an adult (which certainly does require *kabbalat ha–mitsvot* by the convert) the conversion of a minor certainly does not require acceptance of *mitsvot*, but may be done with the consent of the rabbinical court–*al da'at bet din (Shulhan Arukh, YD* 268:7). While the exact parameters of what this means is subject to significant dispute, R. Feinstein actually posits the most liberal view–that since it is always better to be a Jew, every child is eligible for conversion even if they will not be religious upon becoming an adult.[19]

Others contend that such a policy of conversion would be unwise, but it seems at least reasonable that once the conversion of a minor is done by a valid *bet din*, it is always a valid conversion.[20] Under this type of a conversion program, all children of parents who identify as Jewish and wish to have their children raised as Jewish (even if the parents themselves are not halakhically Jewish) would simply have their children converted to Judaism by a *ger katan* program (and perhaps would be expected to send their children to the mamlakhti dati school system).[21] Over the course of a generation, this type of program could potentially solve the current crisis developing in Israel.

NOTES

1. See for example, "Mentally Disabled Citizenship Applicants and the Meaningful Oath Requirement for Naturalization," 87 California Law Review 1017, 1054 (1999).
2. See, for example, Zvi Zohar, "Halakhic Conversion of Non–Religious Candidates," www.jewishideas.org/responsa/halakhic–conversion–of–nonreligious–candidates.
3. This distinction has already been noted by the *Maggid Mishneh*, who comments that the proper distinction to be drawn in Maimonides is between requiring acceptance of the commandments and simply informing the convert of the commandments. See also *Hemdat Shlomo* 29, 30 who explicitly draws this distinction.
4. For example, in *Hilkhot Issurei Biah* 12:17, when Maimonides summarizes post–conversion status, he states "Every gentile when they convert to Judaism and accept all the *mitsvot* in the Torah .... They are like newborn Jews for every matter." We do agree that Maimonides may not require actual performance of the *mitsvot* as a necessary component for conversion *be–diavad*, as is seen from the wives of Samson and Solomon who seemingly never ceased worshiping idols.
5. The original line in the *Bah* reads: "*u–ke–shehayu shelosha be–tevilah af al pi she–lo hayetah le–shem kabbalat ha–mitsvot kol ikar.*" There is sonic ambiguity in how to read "*le–shem.*" It could be read with a *tseirah* (*"le–shem"*), meaning "for the purpose of." In this read, the *Bah* says that Rambam does not require immersion for the sake of *kabbalat ha–mitsvot*. Alternatively, it can be read with a *kamats* (*"le–sham"*), meaning "there," or "at the time of conversion." In this read, the *Bah* is stating that the immersion is valid, even though there was no *kabbalat ha–mitsvot* at the time of immersion.
6. See Encyclopedia Talmudit (vol. 6, page 440 at text accompanying note 233 s.v. *Geirut*), which reflects our read of the *Bah* by stating, "There are those who hold that for *kabbalat ha–mitsvot*, even though three judges are required *ab initio*, nonetheless, if there were three present at the immersion, the conversion is valid, even though there was not at the time of immersion any acceptance of the *mitsvot* at all." See also *Iggerot Moshe YD* 2:127 and *Piskei Din Rabbanim* 10:193, File 1016.
7. Consider for example, the view of *Melamed le–Ho'il* 12:87, where R. Hoffman considers the possibility that Rambam accepts conversion without *kabbalat ha–mitsvot* after the fact, but in the end he concedes that "I do not have the time now to fully consider the matter." See also, *Heikhal Yitshak* (Herzog) EH 1:13 sv. *Ve–hinei ha–Rambam; Divrei Yatsiv* (Halberstam) EH 102; *Tsits Eliezer* (Waldenberg) 15:66.
8. We suspect that in fact it is the view of both Maimonides and *Tosafot* that the four requirements for conversion–sacrifice, circumcision, immersion, and acceptance of the *mitsvot*–can each be waived in a situation in which they are factually impossible. That is why *kabbalat ha–mitsvot* is not required for a minor, circumcision is not required for a man with no penis, and the bringing of a sacrifice is not required in a Temple–less era. We could imagine a case where such could be true for immersion as well as a matter of halakhic theory (although the factual impossibility of immersion is quite rare) at least according to *Tosafot*, although such a case might be subject to a more complex halakhic analysis as the view of Rambam is that the immersion is the central judicial ritual. Although we have no source to prove this, logic would indicate that immersion according to Rambam is no different than acceptance of commandments according to *Tosafot*, and thus when impossible, can be waived–just as the obligation to bring a sacrifice is waived. This footnote raises a number of complex issues and will be, we hope, the subject of a future Hebrew article.
9. Indeed, this terminology comes up frequently in reference to conversion. See, e.g., *Sanhedrin* 96b; *Shabbat* 31a; *Nedarim* 32a.
10. The closest pre–modern halakhic authority we can find who seems to parse the *Yevamot* and *Demai sugyot* in some sort of tension is *Responsa Tuv Tam Ve–da'at, Hilkhot Gerim* 111 (at page 38), which is cited by R. Y. H. Henkin in *Bnei Banim* 2:36. R. Kluger resolves this tension by positing that *kabbalat ha–mitsvot* is merely a rabbinic obligation required for conversion. This view is very far from normative (indeed, we can find no others who agree with this analysis). In fact, even according to the view of those few *Ahronim* who ponder (but do not rule) that Maimonides does not void a conversion done without *kabbalat ha–mitsvot* after the fact, this itself seems to

acknowledge the basic unity of the two sources. Both *sugyot* are normative, this view claims, and should be followed in all cases. It is only after the fact that that one *sugya* is deemed more important than the other. No halakhic decisor rejects the *Demai sugya* as Zohar and Sagi claim.

11. See *Iggerot Moshe* YD 1:157, 1:159, 1:160, 2:124, 2:127, 3:90, 3:106, 3:107, 3:108, 3:112, EH2,:4, 4:16.

12. R. Feinstein's responsa are replete with nuanced analysis of the relationship between full *kabbalat ha–mitsvot* followed by an incomplete shemirat hamitsvot–but it is clear that he requires full acceptance. See Menachem Finkelstein, *Ha–Giyyur–Halakha U–Masseh* 119–24, 356–60 (1994, Bar Ilan University Press, Ramat Gan, Israel).

13. For more on this, see note 9.

14. R. Ben Tzion Uzziel's view is complex and somewhat contradictory. He lays out three views in his responsa, each of which he appears to endorse. One view is that conversion is proper if the convert undergoes a regular *kabbalat ha–mitsvot* even if the *bet din* in charge of the conversion knows that the convert does not actually intend to observe Jewish law. The second view he accepts is that the convert does not actually have to accept that *mitsvot* are binding on him but does need to acknowledge that he understands that the rabbinical court has told him that Jewish law states that he will be punished for his violations of Jewish law. The third view is that the act of immersion is itself a *pro-forma* minimal *kabbalat ha–mitsvot* (this is the view that Sagi and Zohar accept as correct). See *Mishpetei Uzziel* YD 2: 48–55 for his many responsa on this topic.

15. R. Moshe Feinstein, although he rejects the specific conclusion of R. Hoffman with regard to this specific matter, puts forward a very similar rationale which is worthy of thought. He suggests that in modern times, given the general lack of observance of halakha in the Jewish world, it is possible that a convert might genuinely convert to Judaism with a sincere acceptance that Jewish law is binding while honestly thinking that the manner in which Orthodox Jews observe Jewish law is merely a stricture and not actually required by Jewish law. R. Feinstein ponders the possibility that such a conversion is completely valid, as the convert intends to keep Jewish law, but merely does not understand the content of Jewish law. See *Iggerot Moshe* YD 1:160 where R. Feinstein considers this view.

16. Shmuel Shilo, *Halakhic Leniency in Modern Responsa Regarding Conversion,* 22, Israel Law Review, 353, 353–64 (1988).

17. We see no reason to argue that Jewish law intrinsically mandates uniformity on standards of conversion (as it, for example, does on matters of Jewish divorce). Although at first blush one could argue that conversion, like divorce, are core status matters which thus demand a consensus. This is a mistaken read of the reasons why consensus developed in matters of divorce. In matters of divorce, possible *mamzerut* likely develops after a woman is given a divorce that is valid according to one view but not according to others and that possible illegitimacy is essentially uncorrectable. That is not the case in matters of conversion. A person who converts according to one understanding of halakha (which is rejected by other *poskim*) might not be Jewish according to all decisors, but the process of correcting that problem is relatively simple if the parties wish to correct it. For this reason, there has been no firm rabbinic tradition of consensus in many areas of status changing halakha such as conversion or *halitsa*.

18. Our proposal in this section is not new or novel to us. It has been noted in print by R. Jack Simcha Cohen, *Intermarriage and Conversion: A Halakhic Solution* (Hoboken, 1987)–note, as well, the approbation of R. Moshe Feinstein in this work. One of these authors recalls hearing a *shiur* containing this proposal while a student at Yeshiva University, although after these many years it is difficult to recall who gave the *shiur*.

19. R. Feinstein's view is difficult to understand, but we think that the explanation is as follows: R. Feinstein avers that every person is better off being Jewish, but since conversion to Judaism generally requires acceptance of *mitsvot*, and most people, even if they wanted to be Jewish, are not in fact prepared to accept *mitsvot*, the vast majority of people cannot convert. Indeed, the sinning associated with violating Jewish law once one is Jewish makes conversion a bad idea for many people. Minors, however, can only benefit from being Jewish since they can not sin (as they are minors) at the time of their conversion, whereas the theological benefits of Judaism accrue to them immediately even as they are not obligated in *mitsvot*. Obviously, underpinning R. Feinstein's view is the assumption that the rabbinical court need only determine whether the conversion is of benefit to this child at this very moment without pondering into the uncertain

future, a view which seems to be consistent with the general parameters of the rules of *zakhin le-adam she-lo be-fanav*. For more on this issue, see "*Zakhin le-adam shelo be-fanav*," Encyclopedia Talmudit 12:135–197. This issue is worthy of further analysis.

20. The conversion of a minor child is inherently different–as we have noted a number of times in this review, there clearly can be no obligation that a minor child accept *mitsvot*, rather, his conversion is done with the consent of the rabbinical court. No less than four views can be found on when a rabbinical court ought to consent. The first view is the view of R. Kook (*Dat Kohen Milah ve-Gerut* 147–148, and a similar view is taken by R. Elyashiv in *Kovets Teshuvot YD* 2:55) that a *bet din* ought not to convert a child to Judaism unless it is fairly certain that the child will grow up to be religious. The consent of the rabbinical court is a substitute, in this view, for the consent of the child, and no person would consent unless they expect to actually be observant. The second school of thought is that of R. Hayyim Ozer Grodzinski who also advises not to perform such conversions unless the child will grow up to be religious, but recognizes that there will be situations where a conversion can still be validly done even if the children will not grow up observant (see *Ahiezer* 3:28). The third view is the initial view of R Moshe Feinstein, which permits conversions when the child will attend an Orthodox school, since in such a case it is likely that the child will be religious. The final view is the concluding view of R. Feinstein, which is that it is always better for a person who is not obligated in *mitsvot* to be Jewish and thus the conversion of any minor child is valid. (For both of these views, see *Iggerot Moshe* EH4:26(3) and see also *Iggerot Moshe* YD 1:158).

R. Ovadiah Yosef indicates agreement with the first view of *Iggerot Moshe* in his *Yabi'a Omer* EH 2:3 and 2:4. R. Joseph B. Soloveitchik adopted a view that reaches the same conclusion as the most liberal view of R. Feinstein, albeit with a completely different mechanism (*kibush*); see R. Joseph B. Soloveitchik, "Community, Covenant and Commitment" at pages 21–22. (2005) These authors have been told that some halakhic authorities have argued that conversions done according to Rabbis Feinstein and Yosef's view are not accepted even after the fact as valid by those who ascribe to R. Kook and R. Elyashiv's view, although we are aware of no published writings where this is explicitly stated. See *Be–Mareh Ha–Bazak* 1 page 140 n.3 which is contradicted by *Be–Mareh Ha–Bazak* 5 page 179 n.4. It might well be that which view one adopts depends on whether one thinks that such children can, in fact, reject the choice of Judaism made for them as children–when they become adults. For more on this, see *Shulhan Arukh YD* 268:7 and commentaries *ad locum*.

21. We are, to be frank, uncertain if such a program is needed in the United States at this time. Jewry in America is quite aware of the presence of significant numbers of gentiles in America and thus has not developed a need for this type of a conversion program, which can certainly be construed as far less than ideal.

Michael J. Broyde and Shmuel Kadosh

AVI SAGI AND ZVI ZOHAR
A REJOINDER TO BROYDE AND KADOSH

In extensive sectors of our religious community, it is common to regard many things as "obviously true." This affects how people read halakhic texts: assuming that the way we see things today is how religious Jews always saw things, we decide what earlier sources must have –or could not have – meant. When we began work on what ultimately became our book, *Transforming Identity*, we too were quite sure that the current way of understanding *giyyur* was "obviously true." But we decided to adopt the methodological ideal of "suspending judgment," to do our best to read the sources carefully without assuming ahead of time what they must be (or could not be) saying. That is why our book is replete with quotes from hundreds of sources, most of which were never available to readers of English–and many of which are never studied, even by most rabbis. We didn't want anybody to agree with us because "we said so." We wanted to encourage our readers to go back to the sources, to open books they may have overlooked, to consider how interesting and how variegated are the voices of halakhic authorities over the ages–and to appreciate that what seems "self evident" today is but a small segment of the full arc of halakhic approaches that exist in the texts. To succeed in understanding the meaning *giyyur* implicit in halakhic texts, we followed the discussion as it unfolded from rabbinic times to the present. Our project was to write a chapter in the intellectual and cultural history of halakha, to enable the readers to follow the course of the "river of halakha" on this matter, without any pre–judgment as to what "must have been".

In contrast, Broyde and Kadosh (B&K) defend what they take to be the correct religious view of *giyyur*. They do not derive this view from the texts themselves, but come to the sources pre–programmed. Our book, assuming as it does an open horizon of halakhic interpretation, goes against the grain of their orientation. Their "review" of our book is basically a confession of their total devotion to a specific dogmatic view.

B&K read halakha backwards from what appears to them currently as self–evident they infer what earlier sources must have–or could not have–meant. Their writing is replete with assumed premises that prevent them from reading the sources "from within." Current issues are so loud in their ears that they cannot listen to the voice of the texts–nor to our own explanation of what we were doing. Let us give some examples.

As every student of halakha knows, a prominent characteristic of halakha is its "double standard": *le-khat'hilla and be-diavad*. *Le-khat'hilla* defines the halakhic ideal, while *be-diavad* defines the irreducible core of the matter. This duality is very prominent in the realm of *giyyur*. Many rules and guidelines

103

that characterize an ideal *giyyur* do not apply when a situation is characterized as *be–diavad*. In our book we state repeatedly that we seek to explicate not the ideal but the core meaning of *giyyur,* by analyzing what each *posek* defines as the minimum requirements needed to effect a valid *giyyur.* Whatever elements the *posek* leaves out of that definition –however noble and worthy they may seem to us–are, in his view, in the realm of *le–khat'hilla.* It is a logical fallacy to assume that a text discussing *be–diavad* requires anything beyond what it states.

But this is precisely what B&K do over and over again. Thus they claim that *kabbalat ha–mitsvot* is a core *be–diavad* requirement for Hazal–although the Talmud does state explicitly what the minimum requirements for a valid *giyyur* are, and *kabbalat mitsvot* is not included. B&K claim this also with regard to the many *Rishonim* who don't include *kabbalat ha–mitsvot* in the very specific *be–diavad* requirements they do enumerate. B&K's misreading of *Hilkhot Issurei Biah* 13:17 is typical. Rambam explicitly states that (*be–diavad*) if a *giyyur* consisted of circumcision followed by immersion in the presence of three laymen–that is enough for the *giyyur* to be valid. B&K are unable to read this at face value and feel compelled to attribute to Rambam a requirement he could have stated as a *be–diavad* requirement–but didn't: *kabbalat ha–mitsvot.*

Another assumed premise stated outright by B&K relates to the meaning of the terms *hoda'at mitsvot* and *kabbalat ha–mitsvot.* B&K define these meanings (p. 84–85) and then read the texts through the prism of that definition. This blinds them to the possibility that different *poskim* may use the same terms, but interpret them differently. In contrast, we do not assume any *a priori* meaning of these terms, but always do our best to infer the meaning from each *posek's* usage. This enables us to recognize that there exist multiple meanings of the term *kabbalat ha–mitsvot* in halakhic sources–meanings that we present and discuss in part III of *Transforming Identity* (pp. 221–25 1).

Since B&K have such a clear and certain premise about the nature of *giyyur,* they are unable to appreciate a major metaphor the sources use to characterize *giyyur* – "Entering under the Wings of The *Shekhina.*" Though they are aware that this "possibly defines the *geirut* process" and that it "carries with it theological connotations," they immediately jump to the determination (p. 92) that "the phrase entering under the wings of the *Shekhina* conveys a sense that conversion involves a commitment to religious praxis (similar to 'the yoke of heaven')." Given B&K's pre–programmed certainty about the nature of *giyyur,* they seem to have been forced to this arbitrary link of "Entering under the Wings of the *Shekhina*" and entering into a yoke. In contrast, while we too recognized the centrality of this metaphor, we did not pre–determine what it means. Rather, we set about examining the metaphor's usage, paying special attention to Ruth–the source of this usage in the context of *giyyur.* This close reading enabled us to appreciate the following:

> In biblical parlance, "wings" can refer both to parts of a body and to parts of a garment. Both meanings can be relevant in this case: God can be seen as a mighty eagle protecting the Israelites under His wings (ef. Psalms 91:4) or as a powerful male figure taking the people of Israel under the wings of His

Michael J. Broyde and Shmuel Kadosh

garment as His bride. Indeed, the second meaning is found in the book of Ruth itself; when Ruth asks Boaz to "spread the wings of thy garment over thy handmaid" i.e., to take her under his husbandly protection. According to the book of Ruth, when a stranger joins the Jewish people, she becomes a member of the Israelite people who are God's bride, and therefore cones under His husbandly protection. (*Transforming Identity*, p. 123)

Only someone with a totally preconceived attitude could identify the above with entering a yoke.

A fourth major premise stated by B&K as guiding their interpretation of the texts was this: "In general, unified theories of halakha are superior to fractured theories." (p. 91) This simplistic prescriptive assumption is at deep variance with what emerges from an unbiased reading of almost all halakhic sources, namely, the phenomenon of *mahloket* as central to halathic discourse (For a recent work on this matter, see A. Sagi, *The Open Canon*, London: Continuum, 2007). It leads B&K to seemingly desperate harmonization when texts seem to conflict. Not surprisingly, such harmonization inevitably concurs with their own prior assumptions about the nature of *giyyur*.

Their characterization (p. 90) of chapter 268 in *Shulhan Arukh, Yoreh De'ah* as "seamless" is a prime example of this–totally disregarding both the clear problems in the text itself and the recognition of the severity of these problems by great rabbis such as R. Meir Posner and K. Shlomo Zalman Lipschitz (See *Transforming Identity* pp. 200–217). B&K's rigid *a priori* assumptions deafen them to an independent reading of the texts themselves; they prefer deconstruction of the texts over respectful listening to the sources as they are.

A central contention of B&K is that our "consistent misreading of sources undermines the basic value of the work itself" (p. 96). They devote many pages of convoluted argumentation to "prove" this–arguments that mostly consist of special pleading or forced *pilpul*. A clear example is their claim that we misread *Bet Meir*. They state that R. Posner suggests the possibility of *giyyur* without *kabbalat ha–mitsvot* only as a *hava amina*. This is absolutely wrong. Rather, R. Posner does the following: Trying to clarify whether a certain woman had possibly fulfilled the minimum (*be–diavad*) requirements for *giyyur*, he analyzes the various positions on this matter. He declares that there are two different irreconcilable positions in the *Rishonim*. The first is that of Rambam, who holds that (*be–diavad*) *giyyur* is valid by immersion before a *bet din* alone, without *kabbalat ha–mitsvot* (*le–ha–Rambam, nir'eh barur de–kabbalat hamitsvot lihud eino po'el geirut klal, ve–ein tsarikh ela le–khat'hila . . . u–le–da 'ato de–ha 'ikkar akh be–tevilah taliah* (Responsa Bet Meir p. 72). R. Posner states that the woman in question is not a *giyyoret* on this view, since while she did immerse, it was without a *bet din*. He then defines a totally different second position–that he attributes inter alia to *Tosafot* and the *Tur*–according to which a *giyyur* can be valid (*be–diavad*) if a person performs *kabbalat ha–mitsvot* in the presence of a court, and later immerses alone. He defines this *kabbalat ha–mitsvot* as a commitment by the *ger* to the court that s/he will immerse for *giyyur* (*le–shittat ha–Tosafot ve–ha–Tur ve–ha–Shulhan Arukh, ikkar kabbalat ha–mitsvot havi be–ma shemekabbla aleha be–beit din lithol le–shem geirut* (Bet Meir, op.cit.). He then concludes

105

that the available testimony does not enable him to rule out the possibility that such a commitment to immerse may have been made by the woman under consideration. Therefore, she may indeed be a Jew, according to this second position.

Unaware of the eternal truths about "unified theories of halakha" held by B&K, R. Posner never attempts to reconcile these two positions, but feels that under the circumstances he must take each into consideration. Furthermore, in contradiction to what B&K attribute to R. Posner, he never declares the woman's *giyyur* invalid; to the contrary, he says that she requires a *get* from the Jew from whom she received *kiddushin*. This completely mistaken reading is typical for B&K's convoluted scholarship, forced by their original biases to labor in service of predetermined conclusions.

At this point, we have already gone well beyond the number of words kindly allotted to us by the *Tradition*. We conclude with an invitation to the readers of *Tradition*: we hope that you are now more inclined to read *Transforming Identity*, to read the original texts, and to decide for yourself where you agree with us and where you don't–and why. Halakha is exciting, open ended, full of a wide variety of rich and deeply meaningful alternatives–all within Torah! Join the conversation!

MICHAEL J. BROYDE AND
SHMUEL KADOSH RESPOND

Professors Sagi and Zohar begin their rejoinder to our review of their book with an *ad hominem* attack on our intellectual honesty. They accuse us of dogmatically reading sources with a "pre–programmed agenda," while they approach the texts with an "open horizon of halakhic interpretation." We confess that they are partially correct. As students of Jewish law we adhere to basic principles of legal interpretation, namely, considering the interpretative history of the text, or precedent. Reliance on precedent forms the bedrock of any legal system. It is not born out of a blind devotion to authority but rather out of a healthy respect for the generations of scholars studying the same text.

A thousand years of interpreting *Yevamot and Demai* by generations of scholars did not uncover the interpretation that forms the intellectual basis for Sagi and Zohar's work–namely that these two sources conflict with one another. Sagi and Zohar claim that these *sugyot* contain two different approaches to conversion, one with *kabbalat ha–mitsvot* and one without. The radical interpretative revolution they suggest was not born out of a newly discovered manuscript with a variant reading or some other significant insight. Rather, what has changed is the advent of secular Jewish identity. We suspect that this change, more than anything, is what compels Sagi and Zohar to ignore a thousand years of interpretative history in reading these texts. Their dual–*sugya* hypothesis has not been suggested in the past thousand years, because, simply put: *it is a poor reading of the Talmudic texts.* Zohar and Sagi seem to have the real agenda here, which is to manipulate the classical Jewish sources to fit the needs of Israeli society.

Tellingly, although our criticism of the dual–*sugya* hypothesis forms the core of our critique of Sagi and Zohar's work, they do not even bother to reply to our critique–perhaps because after all the huffing and puffing about our motives, they too understand that no regular studier of the Talmud would agree with their view.

To repeat what we noted in the review: Sagi and Zohar claim that the Talmud and certain *Rishonim*, in stating the "minimum" requirements for conversion, exclude *kabbalat ha–mitsvot* and therefore, *kabbalat mitsvot* is not required *bi'diaved*. This is wrong. The Talmud clearly articulates a need for *kabbalat mitsvot* in both *Demai* and *Yevamot* 47–48, the two central texts for conversion. Once that requirement for *kabbalat mitsvot* is articulated, it does not need to be repeated each and every time the conversion process is explored. On the contrary, only when a text explicitly waives a requirement do we assume it is not necessary. In fact, Sagi and Zohar suffer from a fundamental misapprehension about how to determine when texts conflict. When one source says "the sky is blue" and the other states that "there are birds in the sky"–the texts arc complementary, not conflicting. Only when both source cannot simultaneously be true–such as when one source says the sky is blue, while the other says it is red–do the sources conflict. So too with *geirut* when *Demai* and *Yevamot* 47–48 explicitly require *kabbalat mitsvot*, while *Yevamot* 46 does not mention it, we assume that the texts complement each other, and do not conflict.

A close reading of Rambam illustrates this point. In 13:4 of *Hilkhot Issurei Bi'ah*, Maimonides writes: "So too in every generation, when a gentile wishes to enter the Covenant and seek shelter under the wings of the *Shekhina*, and he accepts upon himself the yoke of Torah, he needs circumcision, immersion, and the bringing of a sacrifice." In halakha 17 of the chapter, he writes, "A convert whose motives were not investigated or was not informed of the commandments, but was circumcised and immersed in the presence of three laymen, is a proselyte." His failure to repeat the requirement for *kabbalat ha-mitsvot* in 17 does not indicate its waiver. When Maimonides wished to waive a requirement he articulated before, like "informing the convert of the commandments," he does so explicitly. Despite this, as we note in our review, a handful of authorities have contemplated that Rambam is waiving *kabbalat mitsvot be–di'aved* based on Rambam's defense of Samson and Solomon in 13:14, although they do so in the context of disagreeing with Rambam on this matter, and holding that normative Jewish law does not follow him.

We are perplexed by Sagi and Zohar's critique of our definition of *hoda'ah* and *kabbala*. These are fairly simple and unambiguous terms that are easily understood. Absent strong evidence to the contrary, we think that when a *Rishon* says 'informing' he does not mean 'accepting.' This is certainly true for Rambam, who is noted for the legal precision with which he wrote the *Mishneh Torah*. When your best argument is that an easily defined and widely understood term does not really mean what it seems to mean, you bear a burden of proof that Professors Zohar and Sagi have not met.

Just as Sagi and Zohar do not respond to our observation that their read of the Talmudic sources is wrong, they also did not focus on the multiple instances where we contend that they flagrantly misread texts. Instead, they choose to focus on one source, namely the *Bet Meir*. Despite their vocal protests, we maintain that Sagi and Zohar simply misunderstand the *Bet Meir*'s opinion.

In Responsa 12, the *Bet Meir* is asked by R. Shiomo Lipschitz (author of the *Hemdat Shlomo*) about the status of a potential convert. The woman in question was first converted by women who took her to the *mikveh* and informed her of the commandments. Subsequent to this "conversion," she married a Jewish man. When R. Lipschitz discovered this, he was very upset, but ultimately spoke to the woman to determine whether she was a sincere candidate for conversion. Before R. Lipschitz could convert her, she left again, and when she returned, she was now married to a different husband! R. Lipschitz wanted to know whether any of these actions constituted a legitimate conversion, such that she would be considered Jewish and her marriages binding.

After a lengthy discussion, the *Bet Meir* conjectures that R. Lipschitz's discussion with the woman constituted a *kabbalat ha–mitsvot*, "since she certainly accepted to immerse, and there was probably a discussion of some command-ments." (p. 72b) This was based on the *Bet Meir*'s view that a commitment to perform the rituals of conversion and a commitment to perform some com-mandments suffices for *kabbalat ha–mitsvot*. (p. 72b) *Bet Meir* states directly: "According to the *Tosafot, Tur* and *Shulhan Arukh*, who hold that the central obligation is *kabbalat ha mitsvot*... it is clear that they do not require acceptance of all the commandments. Rather an acceptance of some of the command-ments is called *kabbalat ha–mitsvot*." Thus, *Bet Meir* concludes that according to the Rambam, who requires immersion before a *Bet Din*, neither "conver-sion" was valid. However, according to the normative law of the *Shulhan Arukh* "from her second husband, I am inclined to be stringent [and require a *get*] because if there was a *kabbalat mitsvot* before three, then according to *Tosafot* and the *Shulhan Arukh*, even if she immersed alone, the conversion is valid." (p. 73a) It is clear that the only reason the *Bet Meir* ascribes any possible legitimacy to the conversion is because there might have been a *kabbalat mitsvot*. We do not see how this in any way validates the *Yevamot* paradigm. We are confident that this read of the *Bet Meir* is correct, and that Sagi and Zohar's is wrong. As the *Bet Meir* is not easily accessible, we have posted a copy of this responsa on the *Tradition* blog, "Text and Texture" so that people can read the *teshuvah* themselves.

CONCLUSION

We do not criticize Sagi and Zohar for advancing a read of the Talmudic sourc-es inconsistent with the view of contemporary *poskim*; indeed we recognize that the vitality of Jewish law is preserved by such novel insights (*hiddushim*) and in the last issue of *Tradition* one of us presented such an analysis about a different topic. However, the success of such original readings truly depends on the ability of the proponents of such novel theories to show that their read is consistent with the binding Talmudic sources. Professors Sagi and Zohar have failed at that task. Therefore, while their book is certainly an interesting aca-demic discourse, its practical utility in the contemporary halakhic discourse on conversion is severely limited.

CONTRIBUTORS

MARC D. ANGEL is rabbi emeritus of Congregation Shearith Israel, the Spanish and Portuguese Synagogue in New York. He is Founder and Director of the Institute for Jewish Ideas.

J. DAVID BLEICH is a Rosh Yeshiva at Yeshiva University's Rabbi Isaac Elchanan Theological Seminary and holds the Herbert and Florence Tenzer Chair in Jewish Law and Ethics at the Cardozo School of Law.

MICHAEL J. BROYDE is a law professor at Emory University, Founding Rabbi of the Young Israel in Atlanta and a member of the Beth Din of America.

ABRAHAM CARMEL, the first Roman Catholic priest to convert to Judaism in the last thousand years, taught English at the Yeshivah of Flatbush until his death.

SHALOM CARMY Is Professor of Jewish Studies and Philosophy at Yeshiva University and editor of TRADITION.

J. SIMCHA COHEN is rabbi of Congregation Aitz Chaim in West Palm Beach, Florida.

EMANUEL FELDMAN is editor emeritus of TRADITION

SHMUEL KADOSH is an Assistant Attorney General for the State of New York.

AHARON LICHTENSTEIN is Rosh HaYeshiva of the Hesder Yeshivat Har Etzion in Alon Shevut, Israel, and educational director of the Yeshiva University Gruss Kollel in Jerusalem.

S. ZEVULUN LIEBERMAN is rabbi of Congregation Beth Torah in Brooklyn, New York.

SHLOMO RISKIN is rabbi of the city of Efrat in Israel and Chancellor of Ohr Torah Stone Institutions.

AVI SAGI is founder and director of the Interdisciplinary Graduate Program in Hermeneutics and Cultural Studies at Bar Ilan University where he also is a professor in the Department of Philosophy. He is also a Senior Research Fellow at the Shalom Hartman Institute.

MOSHE YERES is Head of The Talmud and Rabbinics Departments at CHAT Richmond Hill campus in Toronto, Canada.

JOEL B. WOLOWELSKY is Dean of the Faculty at the Yeshivah of Flatbush and an associate editor of TRADITION.

ZVI ZOHAR is the Chauncey Stillman Professor of Sephardic Law and Ethics at Bar Ilan University, where he teaches in the Faculties of Law and of Jewish Studies. He is also a Senior Research Fellow at the Shalom Hartman Institute.